DIAMONDS
OF
THE NIGHT

◊

◊   ◊

◊

DIAMONDS
OF
THE NIGHT

The Search for Spirit in Your Dreams

James Hagan

PAGEMILL PRESS

a division of CIRCULUS PUBLISHING GROUP, INC.

BERKELEY, CALIFORNIA

Diamonds of the Night
The Search for Spirit in Your Dreams
Copyright © 1997 by James Richard Hagan.
Cover image: *Landscape with Stars* by Henri-Edmond Cross, The
Metropolitan Museum of Art, Robert Lehman Collection, 1975
(1975.1.592). Photograph © 1987 The Metropolitan Museum of
Art.

Publisher: Tamara C. Traeder
Editorial Director: Roy M. Carlisle
Cover Design: Gordon Chun Design
Interior Design and Poetry: James Hagan
Typography: Adobe Garamond typeface

Library of Congress Cataloging-in-Publication Data
Hagan, James Richard, 1935-
    Diamonds of the night : the search for spirit in your dreams /
James Hagan.
        p.   cm.
      ISBN 1-879290-13-8 (hardcover : alk. paper).
      ISBN 1-879290-12-X (pbk. : alk. paper).
      1. Dreams. 2. Dream interpretation. 3. Spiritual life.
4. Psychoanalysis. I. Title.
      BF175.5.D74H34 1997
      154.6'3--DC21   96-45175 CIP

Distributed to the trade by Publishers Group West
10 9 8 7 6 5 4 3 2 1
99 98 97

For my friend and inspiration

Marie-Louise von Franz

who understood it all,
and passed it on.

ACKNOWLEDGMENTS

THIS BOOK INCLUDES a description, accurate but not always verbatim, of ninety-four actual dreams. Of that number, twenty-one came from sources in the public domain and one was told to me in ordinary conversation. The rest of the dreams are those of clients or others which are contained herein pursuant to the permission of the dreamers. The author gratefully acknowledges the contributions to this book of those uncommon and courageous men and women. They and other clients have provided both the motive force and original source material for this book.

The author also acknowledges the continuing encouragement and assistance of his friend and editor, Roy M. Carlisle, without whose kind attention this book might have remained undone.

Finally, the author specially acknowledges the great gift to this book by the woman who is Annie. As you will see for yourself, Annie is exceptional.

These are all contributions of rare purity, made without gain or self-interest, made simply that others might see another dimension to life, one that has always existed, but has long been ignored.

Author's Note

This is a book for ordinary people, people who do not have a doctorate degree, but who will read and understand. For that reason, the book has been written in plain language, with brevity, without footnotes, and with as little scientific language as possible. This construction has made it impractical to give credit in this book to all those to whom credit may be due.

Parts of the work of Sigmund Freud, Carl Jung, and William Dement are herein briefly described. In addition, Jonathan Winson might have been recognized for having experimentally demonstrated the existence of the unconscious, thus confirming the early deductions of Jung and Freud. Nathanial Kleitman could also be cited for having first begun the study of sleep and dreams at the University of Chicago. The work of many others could as well be recognized.

The failure in this book to give credit to those to whom credit is due is not meant to slight those who are not here cited, nor is it the result of any lack of respect or of scholarship. It is simply a necessary limitation arising from the structure and the purpose of the book. I therefore apologize in advance to all those who might have been mentioned in this book, but were not.

The Prize of Life yields not up
              Unto the Pure,
              Nor to the Pack;

But only to the One who in the Right Way
              Will Endure,
              And not look Back.

When you are crucified upon the cross,
Or in acid hotly steeped,
When you choke on bitter tears
Which you yourself have weeped,
Rail not against the gods,
Instead remember me,
For when the dross is burned away,
Thereby your soul's set free,
And the living meaning of your life
Will flow at last
Into your unsailed sea.

From *The Parable of the Stone*

PICTURES

CONTENTS

Note on Dreams and Commentary

THE DREAMS DESCRIBED HEREIN ARE TRUE. However, the comments on and interpretations of the dreams are the author's and reflect his years of experience with and ideas about psychology. Accordingly, comments herein about the dreams or the dreamer, or about persons related to the dreamer, are not statements of fact, but are the author's assessments, deductions, conjectures, judgments, theories, and opinions.

Gender Note

WHEN I FIRST LEARNED THE ENGLISH LANGUAGE, the masculine pronoun was used to refer not only to the individual male, but also to a person or persons of unstated gender. Since that time, this usage has been sometimes questioned. Accordingly, I have tried to use in this book the appropriate pronoun in all cases or, where fitting, to use both "he" and "she." Sometimes, however, it is a matter of the syllables, the flow of the prose. Therefore, in an effort to preserve the rhythm of the words, I have from time to time relied upon the traditional usage to refer to the unknown person, a person who may be either male or female. I trust that this occasional usage will not offend any reader.

Preface

CLIENTS HAVE ASKED ME MANY TIMES where they might find a single book about the inner exploration in plain and simple language. I have often wished there were one specific book to which I might refer the reader, but there is no such book of which I am aware. There are, of course, many fine books about psychology, including depth psychology and psychoanalysis. However, my clients have found such books to be slow going and not directly relevant to their own experience. As a result, I have tried here to write the book for which my clients have so often asked. This book is, at best, a modest effort. Even so, I am hopeful that some among you may find it to be useful in a time of need.

Because this book includes descriptions of my work with clients, in order to comply with ethical and legal principles and to protect the privacy and the privilege of the clients, some facts about the clients have been omitted or disguised so that they cannot be identified.

This book is both of and for my clients. These are valuable people, people of a special probity. It is the great reward of the analytic practice to work with such brave and dedicated men and women.

JRH

January 15, 1997

The struggle with the dragon

DIAMONDS
OF
THE NIGHT

The Search for Spirit

in Your Dreams

JAMES HAGAN

◊

◊　　◊

◊

I

RING OF FIRE

THE
ULTIMATE ADVENTURE

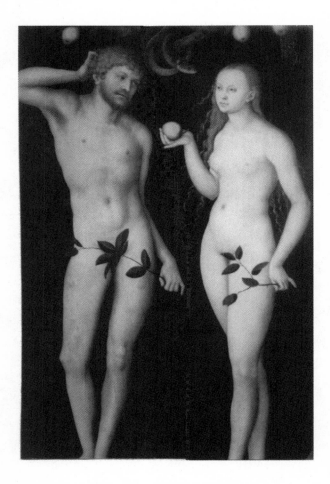

The paradise of ignorance

I

RING OF FIRE

What doesn't kill you
makes you stronger.

Nietzsche

*D*REAMS! This is a book about dreams. About dreams and about the search for spirit within our dreams. And about adventure. The great adventure wherein by means of dreams we explore the world inside ourselves and then the world beyond. The great adventure of a lifetime, but one which all too often begins in fire. Witness this dream which calls a woman to her new adventure.

I awoke to find my house on fire. I ran out, but my dog was trapped inside. Fireman came to fight the fire, but they could not find my dog. So I ran back to save my dog. As I ran toward my blazing house, the fire broke out behind me. Then the fire raced past me on the left. Before I could reach the house, the fire exploded on my right. All of a sudden, I was caught inside a burning ring of fire.

5

This is how dreams look when we are summoned suddenly upon the inner exploration, when life has been remade without our knowledge or consent and we have nothing left to do except adjust to new realities. Life then becomes, indeed, a burning ring of fire. In such event, we might recall with better understanding the words of the great god Krishna:

Fear not to slay that which is already dead.

At such a time we must turn away from a life already dead and walk on within our dreams into the ring of fire. Thus we begin the search for what is yet alive, which also is a search for spirit.

Annie's story, which herein follows, shows us how this great adventure goes. Annie was a young woman in deep distress who cured herself by means of work with dreams. Her story shows us that there is a reason for the fire in life and a purpose for the pain. The point and purpose of the pain is to bring about by force a needed reconstruction. Annie's story shows us how we can stop the pain and move beyond heartbreak and despair when we go to work with dreams. Dreams are the way unto the better day.

We all dream. We know that now without question or dispute. We dream each and every night, four or five times a night. And thus we all exist in two worlds, not one, but two. We live by day in the world of ten thousand things. By night, we wander through the world within, the world of dreams.

We get up from our inner world each day and venture out into that strange external world of danger and delight. We lie down again each night and return in sleep into that nether world inside ourselves, a world of gods and goddesses and fate. And we travel to and through this nether world by means of dreams.

But few of us look at dreams. Few of us know that dreams are quite important, that they are in fact essential to our health, both of the body and the mind. Few of us realize that, if we did not dream, we all would go insane.

But science has at last caught up in part with nature. We know now that dreams occur every day in every human life, that dreams perform a function that is indispensable for every living person. We know now that dreams are the bridge between the worlds, the bridge between the waking world and the world inside ourselves. Without this bridge, this vital link, the human system falls apart or goes awry.

This necessity for dreams applies to us whether we remember dreams or do not. Recalled or not recalled, dreams arise and do their work each and every night. Each and every night from birth to death, dreams flow up from the center of ourselves to acquaint one world with the other, to keep our minds in order, to keep us from becoming too narrow or too bleak.

But dreams are more than mere restraining straps. They serve not just to regulate the system. They have a higher purpose. Dreams enable us to something better in this life, something fine. If we look into our dreams, we see that something wonderful lies within our grasp. Something not quite tangible, something not quite of this world, but something all the same most marvelous. A gift that comes to each of us each night, all wrapped up in dreams.

Dreams transport us each and every night into that strange and radiant world inside ourselves wherein, for better or for worse, we come face to face with powers greater than ourselves. In our dreams, we rise to meet those powers. We rise above the common base material of human flesh and blood and go beyond the whips and scorns of time, the pangs of a despised love, the sickly hue of disaffected resolution. We rediscover joy and appetite for life, we find again creative force.

But dreams cannot accomplish this alone. We must participate. We must work with dreams.

Have you never wondered what would happen if you would remember dreams? I can tell you, as I told Annie, life will change.

When we remember dreams, we find that they have things to say to us. Solemn and substantial things, amazing and astounding things. Things that terrify and things that horrify. And things that guide each life in ways just right for each of us.

And what if we should write down dreams? Then things would *really* change. Dreams written down become concrete, fixed in form and substance. We then can see that dreams are of a grave import, that they tell the story of our lives, but from a different point of view. And we see also that dreams are real, just as real as are events in this external world, but ever so much more vivid and intense, with ever so much more meaning and intent.

And what if dreams become our serious and continuing companions? What if we would welcome dreams, deliberate on dreams, reflect on dreams, ruminate and speculate on dreams, make to understand our dreams? What if we would ingest dreams, digest dreams, absorb our dreams into the living tissue of our very lives? Then our lives are changed forever and for the better.

A doorway opens up. A new dimension beckons. We find inside ourselves a realm both sacred and profane, a brave new world of trial and tribulation, but also of illumination. And here in this unknown world within ourselves, we connect up once again to our own original existence, to that raw and awesome sense of wonder and of reverence that naturally resides inside each one of us.

And what would happen if we had nerve enough to go and peer and probe into that unknown inner world? What if we should be so bold as enter in, walk the land, engage in frank exchange with those that dwell therein?

Then we set our feet on untracked sands. We embark upon an enterprise of greatest pitch and moment, a voyage of vast discovery in the age-old unseen world within.

And what would happen then? How would life change then? Well, we cannot exactly tell. Everything is thereby put at risk, and how in the end the inner exploration will turn out no one can predict. In every life, it is original experience, a case of first impression. There is no map, no chart. It is an undertaking that is discrete and different for each of us according to our own precise design, according to our own peculiar and distinctive gifts. And yet, although we cannot foresee the outcome of the inner exploration, we do know this about the world inside ourselves.

It is rich beyond imagination.

It is the last and final real frontier.

It is the true adventure.

Adventure wherein we cross the arid plain, find water in the well, and slake the thirst, so long unsatisfied, for knowledge of whatever is divine, for spirit and religion.

But we do not discover spirit easily.

We must search for spirit in the unexpected place. Not in any buildings, bricks, or blocks. Not in crystals, stones, or rocks. Nor in any words written down by men or women.

We must search for spirit in the unknown place, in the world inside ourselves, and in the world beyond ourselves. We must search for spirit in the world of dreams, where to our surprise we find it waiting there for us.

This search inside for spirit, this is the ultimate adventure of a lifetime.

This book calls you to that great adventure.

When you have finished with the reading of this book, you will see that you also, no matter what your age or stage of life, if brave enough and resolute, can cross that last frontier, and can yourself achieve this ultimate adventure.

This is the gift of dreams.

This is the gift of dreams.

Now let us look at Annie's dreams as she embarks upon her great adventure. Let us see what we might learn from Annie and her dreams.

◊   ◊   ◊   ◊

2

ANNIE'S STORY — FIRST YEAR

THE
BURNING

The price of our awareness

2

ANNIE'S STORY — FIRST YEAR

In a dark time,
the eye begins to see . . .

Theodore Roethke

ANNIE WAS HER NAME, the name which we shall call her. She had been in an accident in life, and it had left her badly damaged. Her life was in upheaval, full of tumult and turmoil. Pain and heartache were her everyday companions. She was at wit's end. She had nowhere left to turn. Then she heard how dreams might help her in her life, and so she came to me to work with dreams.

This is how the process starts. One is wounded and in pain, and so in desperation turns to work with dreams. In the end, these are the lucky ones among us, for these discover dreams, and dreams will make them well and whole again.

So these dreams that follow, these are Annie's dreams. Dreams that changed her life and made her well once more.

April 7th — Kidnapped
I have been captured by Russians. They take me to a prison ship. I wait in line to go through a chamber filled with poison gas. A man opens up the door and shoves me in. Before I go, I take a deep breath so I don't breathe the gas, then I run through and out the other side where there are other prisoners. A dark man guards this room. He has a long black gun that he points around like he will shoot someone. I am in a line waiting to sit down. The guard puts the gun against my head. I know that he's a little crazy and that he may actually kill me. But he doesn't. Finally, I get to sit down and look around. I see that the ship is anchored in a Russian harbor.

This early dream presents a vivid picture of Annie's poor condition. She has been kidnapped. She has been stolen from herself. No wonder her life is in disarray.

This dream, and Annie's other dreams described in this book, are but a few of her dreams. Annie was an active dreamer. During the period of our work, she and I went through about fifteen hundred of her dreams. The dreams presented here have been selected for their exceptional clarity and power, and because they so well demonstrate the wonderful capacity of dreams for truth and confrontation, for healing and for change. The dreams are quoted more or less verbatim as recorded by Annie, except where they are edited for brevity or to protect the privacy of Annie or of others.

Like most who come to analytic work, Annie came concerned about matters in the outside world. Out there, Annie's life was full of suffering and of chaos. Her relationships were wild and overheated. She lived in fear for health and safety, and for sanity. In short, she had lost control. Everything important in her life had been called starkly into question.

In this rending conflict, Annie thought that her discomfort was all the fault of others. She thought that she would be all right if only others would cease to be a problem. Annie was in this regard quite wrong. She had it backwards. It works the other way around. When we are unsound inside ourselves, we become emotionally addicted to others. Then they can really do us harm. In contrast, when we are well-connected to the life inside, we are not dependent and therefore others do not leave us arrayed around the room in ugly bloody spots. For this reason, serious problems are not resolved by outward effort, but fade away only when the inner discord is diminished. In other words, in order to fix our problems, we have to fix ourselves. This is why we all are made to dream. Dreams disclose to us the inner altercation and provide the means for us to intervene and thereby forge a peace between contending powers.

Like Annie, we are all from time to time caught up in red-hot outer conflict. Such conflict captivates us. We are immobilized. We are in danger, but we cannot get away. It is so intense, so impassioned; it seems to be of such appalling consequence. But this is an illusion. The outer conflict is really just a symptom, and our excessive fascination with what lies outside ourselves blinds us to the inner issue. The root of our discontent festers deep inside. The fault, we find, lies not in our stars, but in ourselves. And so upheaval in our outside life has its value. It is the fire which forces us to look within, and then to go to work with dreams.

Annie's dreams did not address the outside problems which to her were of such consequence. Instead, the dreams addressed internal trouble, and with most dramatic impact. As this first dream shows, Annie had become a captive in a life that was toxic to her. This is the real cause of her travail. The problems in the outside world result from this, not *vice versa*.

This kind of misadventure is not infrequent. As with all of us, Annie was born unasked into this world and was shaped by forces out of her control. Parents, schools, churches, all with good intentions and sure that they were right, imposed rules and expectations upon the unsuspecting child. These rules and expectations deflected Annie's growth, knocked her off her natural path. This was Annie's accident. She was hit by rules and expectations that warped and so distorted life that Annie wandered then in ways that were harmful to her, in ways that were destructive to her life.

This first dream makes clear the task of Annie's inner work. She must declare her independence. She must fight free of her confinement. And with her new found freedom she must find the life that is right for her according to her own original design, according to her individual gifts.

Annie begins this battle at heavy disadvantage. She is already the captive of an evil empire. The only out for her will be by combat. It will not be easy, nor is the aftermath at all certain. Hostile forces once in power do not lightly yield. They battle back with all the rage and cunning of a deadly foe. If she is to have a chance, Annie must be implacable in her efforts, absolutely unrelenting. This struggle for her own existence is an all-or-nothing undertaking. It will stress Annie to the very marrow of her bones and test her will and her resolve to the last ounce of her integrity and character.

If Annie is here both game and honest, she may prevail to independence. But if she falters, if she is not all the way committed, she will be defeated and will end up a permanent prisoner on that terrible ship in her dream. In that case, the pain and chaos she faces now will recur throughout life in endless variations. Accordingly, Annie here has nothing left to lose and everything to gain by opposing her confinement.

As a result of this dream, Annie sees her plight at last and understands her struggle. She begins to grasp the fact that the outcome of this conflict will decide her future. Since all of Annie's adult life lies yet ahead, nothing could be more important to her than that she succeed in this endeavor. By how she here conducts herself, Annie will determine what kind of person she will be and what kind of life she will lead. This is, quite literally, a contest for life or death, a contest played out in Annie's inner world, all by means of dreams.

April 10th — Stormy Weather

I am on a tiny island. A giant tidal wave is about to hit me. In the distance, I see tornadoes forming in the water. Farther out, there is a hurricane, too. I am crouched next to a small unfinished wall. It is not enough to protect me. I am very frightened.

According to the dream, storms are coming. Annie will undergo heavy weather of every kind. Confusion and disorder will flow through her life. She will be in peril of being blown away because she has inadequate protection, that is, she is not yet well-developed. Her protective wall is just too small.

This dream is another one about Annie's inner condition, not about her outside life. The personal details of Annie's life are in these dreams reflected at a minimum. Such details are in the large view unimportant. Although dreams rise in the context of a specific human life, they go beyond the merely personal into the deep interior. The important dreams address internal content and universal values, which are the things that really count in every life. However, just because we do not here discuss the details of Annie's personal life, do not think that it was dormant or suspended. On the contrary, Annie's life was very active. She left a long-time emotional commitment. She moved to a new residence. She changed jobs. And she did all this while grappling with the pain and chaos which we see depicted in these dreams.

As this dream of heavy weather shows, Annie will be going through a bad time. There is no way to bypass what is even now underway. The storms in Annie's life have been already born and wicked this way come. Therefore, the question here for Annie will be one of raw survival. Can Annie hold on until her wall can be enlarged, or will she be blown away by winds of change too strong for her to bear?

As you will see as you read on, this question will be narrowly decided. This early dream of tempest and typhoon was every bit too accurate.

April 25th — Crocodiles

I am at my family home. We are sitting down to a meal in the dining room. To my surprise, there is a pool of water underneath the table, and there are crocodiles in it. We all ignore the crocodiles as if they are not there. Then I must go into the kitchen. In order to do so, I must cross the water to the other side. I sit on the back of one of the crocs and we swim across the water. But then I slip off the crocodile and fall into the water, and the other crocs swarm all around me. But they don't hurt me. I get to the other side of the water and crawl out. Then the crocodiles come after me. They chase me around the kitchen trying to bite me. I hop on the couch to get away. One of the crocs crawls up the back of the couch after me. I push the couch against the wall to crush the crocodile, but it keeps hanging on, still trying to bite me.

This is a dream of invaluable information, and also of disillusion.

At the time that Annie undertook to work with dreams, she was close to thirty years of age. She was an intelligent, educated, attractive person who led a lively social life. She did not abuse drugs or alcohol. She came from a large family, had never been married, had no children, lived in a large city, and was employed and self-supporting. Her original home was stable, except that her father was not there. The family was centered on a mother of some rectitude, a church of rules and dogma, and family obligations. Annie no longer followed in the mandates of the church, but it had left behind in Annie's life deleterious effects. Annie was still tightly tied up to her mother, and the family was dominant in her life. But to her shock and her dismay, this dream tells Annie that her family is not a healthy place. It is a pit of crocodiles. In other words, Annie's family is unsafe for her.

This news is very disturbing to Annie. She loves her family, she has no wish to depart therefrom. But the dream is plain enough. The family setting is dangerous for Annie.

The family is a danger not because it is malicious. The danger is not due to hatred or to ill will. On the contrary, the danger stems from too much closeness and too little understanding.

In the image of the dream, the family setting has become a crocodile-infested bog. This has serious consequences. If Annie stays within the family circle, in a psychological sense, the crocodiles will devour her individual life. For Annie to make her separate life worthwhile, she will have leave this dark and deadly marsh. When in the dream she tries, she falls into the water with the crocodiles. She is afraid, but is not harmed. So long as she remains immersed, she is equally instinctive with the crocodiles and they do not assume to dine on her. But when she leaves the mire, she commits the cardinal sin, the sin of individual ambition. The crocodiles then come after her. As the dream ends, although Annie fights, it is not clear whether she will survive or be eaten by the beasts. But fighting back is an important effort and it gives a good prognosis. If one will fight, then one can win. Therefore, in dreams, you must always fight to save yourself. You must never quit, never yield.

April 29th — The Tenement
I visit a poverty-stricken housing development. In one of the houses lives an old woman with about fifty children.

Dark men who are bill collectors come to her door every day, but she doesn't answer. Her children are dirty and hungry. But they are standing in a group singing to her. One of the girls has an especially angelic face. They all leave one day and I go into the house to take a nap and do my laundry, but the washing machine is dirty and there is no soap. I go back to where I came from and I ask two people who are my superiors for some money to give to this woman and the children. I feel like a missionary. My superiors tell me that the family is not used to having money, and that I must be careful not to do too much for them. My superiors point out that I should consider helping people in my own neighborhood. There are three of them nearby, also very poor. So I go to help them. They see me coming and run away, but then they see that I really want to help, and they come back and embrace me. They are happy to see me at last.

We see here Annie's inner world. It is a mess!

The tenement reflects a deeper level of Annie's internal existence, far from Annie's everyday awareness. She is shown that the world within has been woefully neglected and has become terribly impoverished. Although it is full of future possibilities in the many children which it harbors, it is heavily taxed by the inner masculine presence, the dark men who come every day with new demands. Without her knowledge, Annie has become a slumlord. Even so, there is reason to have hope for Annie's future, for the tenement contains one child who is especially beautiful, and this extraordinary child may become Annie's future.

Annie tries to rest here in her inner world, and to clean up. But the washer is too dirty and there is no soap. In other words, Annie cannot yet work at this deep level. Annie is advised by superior wisdom that she would do better to work closer to home with the more immediate companions in her own neighborhood. She takes this good advice and turns to three nearby neighbors. However, they are afraid of her and run away. After all, Annie has not been to them a friendly face. But this time is different. This time Annie has come to make real and permanent change. Her companions recognize this fact and return and embrace her, overjoyed that Annie has finally understood, that she has come at last to lift them out of their privation and include them in the conduct of their joint life. The four of them now, Annie and her three companions, make up the full array of personality, the four parts of the individual existence of each of us as explained in the definitions that follow this chapter.

This dream marks a turning point for Annie. Now at last complete in her psychology, she may bring prosperity to her tenement and to her inner friends. This is quite important. These inner friends are other aspects of Annie's personality, previously unknown and not developed. They will add a richness and variety to Annie's life that she has not had before. And they will help her. As you will see in later dreams, the added strength and vision of these inner friends is critical. In several dreams that follow, they come to Annie's aid in time of urgent need. Without the help of these companions, Annie would have been at even greater risk in the trials that follow.

May 24th — Chocolates

I am hungry. I go to the refrigerator to get something to eat. But the refrigerator contains no real food. Instead, it is full of Hershey's chocolates and peanut butter treats. There are hundreds of them, stacked everywhere, and there are also many coupons so that I can buy more when these are gone. There is no room for anything else.

This is another dream of startling information. In dreams, we often see chocolate as a synonym for sex, the dark sweetness of life, our reward for the labors of this life. In this dream, we see that Annie has become a little too fond of sex. There is nothing else that feeds her. There is in her life no real nourishment, no love, no true affection, only the dark pleasures of sex which have excluded everything else. This does not work out well. Sex is good, but sex alone is not enough.

Despite the image in the dream, Annie is not a sexual libertine. She does like fun and entertainment, and for entertainment she may from time to time engage in sex without so much emotional attachment. After all, she is a single person in her youth. However, as the dream suggests, sex without more has little lasting value. We can play around a bit in adolescence, but as we age the game begins to change. Life becomes a serious engagement, and sex becomes a serious endeavor.

This dream explains in part the early damage from the family setting. In youth Annie somehow learned that men cannot be trusted. They come for sex and go away too soon. Therefore, so far as Annie is concerned, sex is all there is. Real affection does not exist. Annie feeds on sex because she is ignorant of love. Annie lives on sugar because she does not know that bread exists.

This lack of love has been disastrous for Annie. It has badly misguided her life. In this matter, Annie is not so much an adult making choices about sex. It is more that she is still a child who in youth was injured in an accident which left her partially retarded. This is actually quite accurate. In her emotional life, Annie's accident left her slightly blind, or with distorted vision. She never saw the possibility of love. She is just now beginning to see that she may have a different choice. And with another choice, she can become more responsible in matters of the heart. So Annie has now a chance to change, a chance to live a different life, and perhaps a chance for love.

Like Annie, many of us have accidents in early life. We are just rumbling along as little tykes when some big truck or train runs right over us. It is one thing for me, another for you, a different issue for each of us. Whatever it is, this accident resonates through life and subverts all experience in peculiar ways which we never know or understand. In short, such accidents poison life. We can only escape the consequences of such accidents if at some time we discover what they were and then fight back. We may always bear the scars, but these accidents and injuries need not forever limit life.

July 10th — Sharks
In the distance, I see a storm forming. Then a flood hits. Then I'm swimming with my mother in the ocean.

Some pretty white fish swim with us. I point them out to my mother. One of them comes to the surface. It has a big fin which juts out above the water. I suddenly realize in horror that these are not pretty little fish, but great white sharks. I am scared to death. I begin paddling to get to a place of safety. I'm afraid my movements will attract the sharks and they will bite off my hands. But I keep on paddling anyway with all my might, and I finally reach a place where the ocean runs up against a concrete wall. I grab hold and use my last bit of strength to climb out and get to a safe place.

This dream brings to Annie unpleasant information. It suggests that her mother brings the sharks that are so dangerous, that her mother is the source of family problems. This is most disturbing. For a long time, Annie's mother has been the person who cared for Annie and the family. To her credit, Annie's mother raised the children mostly by herself. She was conscientious; she did the best that she knew how to do. Annie and the other children rely on her and trust her. To find out now that her mother may be unhealthy is a heavy blow to Annie's basic footing. And Annie, too, must bear some blame. She has perhaps relied too much upon her mother.

From this dream, Annie can see what needs to be done. She must get some distance from her mother. In a psychological sense, although she does not mean to be, Annie's mother *is* the shark, the classic case of a devouring parent. She does her best. She does not intend to be sinister, she just cannot help herself. She is not aware of her effects, and therefore she cannot control the unknown elements of life that appear in dreams as sharks. This makes her a hazard to her children.

As the dream reflects, the sharks who swim with Annie's mother may bite off Annie's hands, that is, destroy Annie's competence. This is an actual peril. If in the dream a shark should bite off Annie's hands, the results would show up somehow in the external world. Annie's capacity to manage life would be seriously impaired. She would never be fully self-sufficient. But in the dream Annie sees the danger. She sees that she must leave her mother's waters. This will not be easy. Mothers who cruise shark-infested waters apply abundant powers to bind their children to them. They will, if so permitted, feed on their young forever. Thus will the parent wax while the child will wane. But in this dream Annie gets away. She is able to escape without injury. There is therefore reason to have hope.

Around this time, Annie told me about a dream of another member of her family. This dream concerned a dangerous man within the family home. This other dream came to Annie quite unexpectedly from someone who had no knowledge of Annie's analytic work. For Annie, this dream from another family member was important because it was a confirmation from an independent source that serious problems lay within the family circle. She was able to see that the family affliction was not confined to her, nor did it emanate from her. She was able to see that there was a deviant element in the family dynamic that was dangerous to the children, herself included.

As we have learned in depth psychology, a deviant masculine element in dreams is often an unknown aspect of the mother. (Similarly, a wild and dangerous woman in a dream may spring from the father in the family.) Of course, the mother in this case is not aware of this disorder. Most people are unaware of the inner apparatus and therefore take no responsibility for the life that dwells therein. From ignorance and neglect, the inner life turns sour, festers, and then breaks out and runs amok as has happened here. There is no check upon the damage done because no one sees the wreckage and the ruin.

This is how people are most dangerous. They appear to be so nice, so sweet, so suitable. But they have a dark side about which they do not know. Just like that paragon of virtue, the kindly Dr. Jekyl, all of us have inside a Mr. Hyde (or a Ms. Hyde), and, in a psychological sense, this inner criminal sneaks out at night while we sleep to wreak havoc upon unwitting victims, often undefended children.

The only thing that can be done to limit or restrict such damage is an effort by the mother to recapture and restrain the masculine marauder. She is the only one who can catch him, so everything depends on her. However, since this mother knows nothing of the renegade or his rapacious ways, she can do nothing to protect her children. The children must therefore protect themselves. They must beware the family home. They must get away and stay away. If this seems harsh, the parent must understand that she has a fundamental duty to be aware of her condition, and to protect her children from her own internal darkness. And the children have a right, a duty to themselves, to be immune from such onslaught. After all, children suffer more than enough in early life from well-meaning parents. Accordingly, as adolescents and adults, they must assert themselves. To save themselves, they must avoid the family home wherein the demons dwell. And if they have children of their own, they must keep them far away from the ministrations of the mother. Otherwise, they may unwittingly transmit the family damage to their own offspring.

August 31st — The Crash

I'm taking two young boys out to get something good to eat. They are in the back seat of my car. I'm driving uphill pretty fast when I come to a dead end. One of the boys yells at me to slow down because I'm going to hit the wall. But I stop before I do and tell them I'm right where I want to be. There's a store on the left that sells all kinds of good food. I'm going in to get us something. I back up to parallel park. As I do, the rear wheels of the car drop into a deep hole. I put the car into first gear to go forward, but when I accelerate the sudden force flips the car over. The car starts to slide downhill. It goes faster and faster and spins around. I'm trying to get to the keys to turn the engine off, but I can't reach them because I'm being thrown about. Finally, I reach the keys and turn the motor off. I say to myself, "Please don't let my nice car crash." But we're about to hit a wall. I try to stop the car by holding out my hands. It doesn't work. We hit the wall hard. My car is badly damaged, and I am hurt. It's very

*quiet in the back and I'm afraid the boys are hurt. Then I
see myself in the mirror. My face is bloody from many cuts.
My left arm is broken in half at the elbow. The bones stick
out of my flesh, and I am covered all over in blood. I have
a car phone so I call 911, but I don't dial right. I try again
and get it right this time. They answer and I tell them
there's been an accident and please send help. Then I pass
out from shock and loss of blood.*

This is what occurs when we violate our own
imperatives. We hit a wall. We have a bad crash.

What happened here is this. Annie had a relapse.
She got hungry for sweets again, and she took a little
bite. That is, she had a little party and a little sex without emotional attachment. But to her dismay, she
found penalty instead of pleasure. She found that her
defiance of her own nature constitutes betrayal, and
that betrayal carries with it a terrible reprisal.

Since the dream about the chocolates, Annie had
restrained herself. She has had a simple rule: *No love,
no sex.* This is a very good rule, one which to our
advantage we might all maintain. But a part of Annie
likes adventure. A part of Annie likes to drink a little
and dance a lot. And maybe have a little sex. Sex is,
after all, an addictive drug, and it is hard to stop. So

Annie decided to feed the young men inside herself, to give them some amusement one more time. She took them out for food and stopped at what she thought was just the right place. But Annie found that one more time was one time too many, and that this road to fun was actually a dead end.

Annie offended her inner sense of what was right for her. She ignored the internal demand for change in her attitude regarding sex. She indulged herself once more. And she received an immediate response. This dream made it perfectly plain in most dramatic form that Annie had done serious damage to herself and that sex without affection is a poison in Annie's life.

A dream like this is so clear that one need not be a scientist to see the meaning. Annie saw it right away and responded right away. She resolved to sin against herself no more. This was Annie's last surrender to the lure of sex where love was not also present.

In Eastern religions, self-indulgence is the great offense. Annie's dream reminds us that this is also true even here in our modern Western world.

Annie's crash tells us something else as well. From this dream we learn that there are principles that permeate our lives, that there naturally reside inside each of us ideals of what is right and what is wrong.

We learn that we ignore this inner sense of right and wrong at our peril.

This is most important. In work with dreams we see within the human heart transcending human values that are constant over time. This is especially true regarding love and sex. In all the dreams that I have seen where sex has been an issue, even in this liberated age and in both men and women, sex without emotion has always been condemned. Only sex in service to affection seems to be approved.

October 7th — Suicide

I am in despair. I decide to kill myself. I insert two steel spikes into each side of my face. They staple down beneath my chin and will kill me pretty soon. I get into my car and drive down the freeway waiting to die. I feel the life drain out of me. Then it occurs to me that, if I die while driving, I may crash and hurt an innocent person. So I stop at a roadside restaurant. I go into a restroom to wait until I die. I go into a stall and lie down on the floor. As I lay dying, I reflect upon my life. I realize that I have my whole life ahead of me, and that my feeling of despair is only a temporary condition. It will pass and things will get better. Now I don't want to die, but I am too weak to save myself. Just then my sister comes into the restroom. I have very little strength left, just enough to call to her for help. She sees what I have done, and she pulls the spikes out of my face. The pain is awful. I feel the tissues tearing in my skin. I am in agony, but I start to recover. My sister comforts me. She tells me that I was close to death, and that I couldn't have saved myself alone.

Annie has encountered the clash within herself. Demand for change collides with her reluctance, with her comfort and complacence. The conflict is intense. It exceeds Annie's efforts. So Annie gives up and seeks escape in death rather than to be responsible in life.

Annie is too committed to the family home, and to the pleasures of the flesh. She cannot let go of what she has to move on to what will be. She is stuck. This is a dangerous condition, and it brings Annie to a crisis. The outcome of all her efforts in this inner work will hinge upon her decisions in this matter.

Sooner or later, all who engage in the inner exploration come to a similar conflict. All who hear the call to make a better life must at sometime leave old ways behind and leap into an unknown future. It is a difficult decision, one fraught with pain and peril.

At this point, we do not know what Annie will decide to do. Even though some dreams have implied that there is something special up ahead for Annie, she may not get there. She is still caught up in the struggle to change the way she lives. If Annie will not make the change, then all the promise of the future will be lost, will turn to dust and blow away.

Annie's task is well-defined. Dreams have shown her that the road ahead requires separation from her family and new attitudes regarding sex. But Annie is not quite ready. She finds it difficult to give up casual sex, and she finds it hard to break away from the family circle. The family is close, and family values are maintained by convention, church, and Hallmark cards. Annie is loyal, she is congenial, she has no wish to be a problem. She is part of the glue that holds the family pattern in its place. But Annie is now subject to contradictory demands. Her individual life demands that she move out alone and on her own, and with some principles. These two great imperatives, family values and individual life, they oppose each other. Annie does not see how she can make the change that dreams demand, and yet she knows that she can no longer live as in the past. She is wracked by inner discord.

This has always been the great danger. We have never known whether Annie was committed all the way. The inner life makes demands that few of us find easy to accomplish. Even so, one is expected to be strong enough to stay the course.

We now can see the meaning of Annie's dream. At the beginning, death seems preferable to the bitter battle that is underway. In a terrible attempt to end her misery, Annie drives spikes into her face to kill her new awareness. However, even here Annie remains typically considerate. She leaves the freeway so that she will not do injury to others. What a nice person! She protects the innocent even while in the throes of death. She elects to assassinate herself rather than to be a problem to her family.

Like a wounded creature, Annie crawls into a bathroom stall to find a private place to die. But then she is attacked by a subversive thought. At her last discerning moment, Annie realizes that suicide is not correct. She sees that her problems will not last. This is a time of hard transition, but it is not a permanent position. If she will see things through, if she will just hang on a little longer, she has a life ahead. But she is now too far gone to fix herself. She needs help, and perhaps help will come. After all, God loves courage, and Annie now has companions of the world within who watch over her. And sure enough, an inner sister comes again to Annie's aid. With everything at issue, Annie is not yet strong enough. She still needs help from inner friends. And inner friends make all the difference. With their help, Annie makes it through the peril, survives each close call. But without help from inner friends, Annie's life would go awry and wither on the vine.

In respect of Annie's great despair, we all at times encounter such heartache. Life is sometimes just too much for us. But we all have inner friends. If we call, they will come and pull us through.

Annie's dream illustrates another hazard of this life, the great evil of refusing hard decisions.

Nature asks everything of us, but never more than we can bear. We are not pushed beyond our limits, but we are pushed up to our limits. And within those limits we are expected to do what is required, to make the difficult decision. There are consequences if we do not. By a failure of courage or of commitment, we may unleash against ourselves relentless force which seeks to do us in because we are unfit. By hesitation, even more by indecision, we mark ourselves unworthy, and then the life inside becomes destructive. If we fail to make the necessary choice, we let loose all the demons of the night upon ourselves, and life simply comes apart.

In this regard, witness poor Hamlet. He did not make the necessary choice and so let loose havoc and destruction on everyone around, himself included and even poor Ophelia. But we need not repeat such error. We have dreams whereas Hamlet only had a ghost. In our dreams, we can see the imperatives inside. We can see the duty to do the best we can with what we have while we are here. We can see that we must choose not what is cheap or easy, but what is right. It is in this choosing that we define our lives. Penalties accrue for cowardice. Rewards await the brave.

November 27th — Murder

I am driving down a freeway. It narrows down and turns into a two-lane road. Several cars come speeding toward me. I almost drive into a ditch to avoid collision. A car ahead of me breaks down. The driver is another girl about my age who is wearing a red jacket. I stop to lend a hand. One of us will have to go for help. But suddenly a fat and furious woman attacks the other girl. The girl pushes her away. Then the raving woman turns on me. She knocks me down and leaps on me. I am helpless in her hands. Then two policemen come. They pull her off of me and take her to a bench. She sits down and seems to go to sleep. I get up and thank the policemen for saving my life. We talk and then they leave. Suddenly the raging woman wakens. She attacks me once again, knocks me down

again, and bites and tears my throat. She is completely
mad. I fight her, but she does terrible damage to me. I
realize that I am losing lots of blood. I lay there on the
ground, helpless as I watch my life's blood drain away.

This is a very bad dream. It is a backlash to Annie's
analytic work. The raging woman is the dark side of
Annie's life. She is fat, a sign of Annie's earlier self-
indulgence. She has been driven wild by Annie's
progress in her analytic efforts. Annie's new awareness
threatens this raging woman's power. She is resolved to
do away with Annie before Annie does away with her.

This dream tells an important story. As Annie
speeds along life's highway, her options narrow down
and she confronts colliding values. Annie's feeling life,
the woman in red, breaks down. Annie stops to give
assistance, as she should. But before help can come,
Annie's feeling life, and Annie in her turn, are attacked
by Annie's own dark side. Fortunately, elements of
order come to Annie's aid. The two policemen disable
the raging woman for awhile. But even they do not
appreciate the threat she represents. Annie is at greater
risk than anyone anticipates, and the police depart too
soon. So this psychotic woman has another chance. She
attacks again and this time throws Annie down, pins

her to the ground, and rips out Annie's throat. She is desperate to abolish Annie's fresh new life before it can consolidate, before it can take control away from her. Annie lies there helpless as her life bleeds away.

This dream depicts the dreadful menace of an inner enemy. When Annie decided to become aware and to change her life, the clash between the two became inevitable. As earlier observed, inner figures once in power do not accept demotion. They fight back with deadly force. Therefore, if you should choose to do the inner exploration, you must be prepared to kill or die. There is no halfway measure. It is a matter of survival. It is the question of who will govern life. Will the renegade win out, or will you prevail? Will you regain your life, or will you lose it? In every case, it is life or death within the dreams.

This dream of Annie does not end well. She is in real trouble, at a point of maximum peril. At such a time as this, we who stand with Annie in her battle can do little except to wait and hope. And pray for strength. And pray for grace.

Thus ends the first year of Annie's analytic work. It was a hard year for Annie, and its conclusion is somewhat problematic. Annie's dreams were difficult for her.

They demolished her sense of safety in her family. They criticized her conduct. Given a free choice, Annie would surely have skipped this rugged education. But Annie did not have a choice. Her life had come apart and to save herself she had to undertake this agonizing self-examination. For Annie, this work with dreams was utterly essential.

Work with dreams sometimes becomes essential for others, too. When we encounter trouble in our lives, when we are unhappy or dissatisfied, how can we know what we should do unless by means of dreams we look into the life inside? Without our dreams, how can we find out what unknown force corrupts our lives? And if we do not find out, how can we take up arms and by opposing bring an end to our affliction?

We can do so only when we open up to dreams and see what truth they have to tell. Truth is the invincible weapon. No matter how hard the truth may be to bear, if we can see what is true about our lives, then we can make a choice and we can save ourselves.

But knowledge of the truth does not come without a cost. The truth can put us all into a most deplorable position, For when we see the truth, we then become responsible. When we *can* make a choice, we *must* make a choice.

This is now where Annie stands. She has seen the truth about her life, and she must make a choice. But the choice is not easy. Annie must choose between her family and her future. She must choose between what feels good and what is good. She must choose between what is pleasant and what is right. And which of these she chooses will make all the difference in the person she will be.

So at the anniversary of Annie's inner exploration, we can only wait and wonder: What will Annie do?

Will she choose a life
of promise and potential?

Or will she by her choice cast herself
into the outer darkness?

◊   ◊   ◊   ◊

3

THE ANALYTIC EFFORT

Inward
Exploration

The evil of the female

3

THE ANALYTIC EFFORT

Exultation is the going
of an inland soul to sea . . .

Emily Dickinson

ANNIE'S ANALYTIC WORK was her reprieve. Without the work, she would never have known that she was on the road to her ruin, that the way she was living was also her doom. She would never have seen that she had many other options, that better possibilities did beckon. Without the analytic work, those better possibilities might have been forever lost in the mists of time, a tragedy for Annie and also for all those others who cross her path in this lifetime.

Work with dreams saved those better possibilities for Annie. However, as she found out, work with dreams is not an gentle labor. It can be a heavy and a bitter task. It tests your mettle to the last degree. It strips the bones and bakes the flesh. But it takes you to surprising places, and it leads to revelation. It is sore ordeal. It is also grand campaign.

The Split Inside

The internal exploration is the messy and uncertain means by which we modern men and women reconstruct ourselves inside. We usually come into this work only when propelled by pain. Pain is therefore a gift. It is the engine of wisdom. And pain is a testing, a filter used to sift the human congregation. It tempers and refines. It is a catalyst that when applied to some of us yields a new creation. So when and if we find ourselves wracked by the pain of strong emotion, injured in the lists of life, we ought not weep and run away. Instead, we should rejoice. We should take comfort that the pain will take us where we need to go, and that it will yield a good outcome.

But pain has its dangers. It can devour all our basic faculties, and it can kill. So the first concern in analytic work is to arrest the rush of pain, stem the flow of blood, alleviate the suffering. This is, however, only the beginning. The real work lies beyond the pain.

So the telling point is always this: How do we respond to pain?

Therein lies the problem, for ofttimes we ourselves are split inside and so respond to pain in woeful ways. But the pain is actually a calling. It calls on us to heal the split so thus to heal ourselves.

And we heal this split by means of dreams.

Then something wonderful will happen. When we heal the split inside ourselves, the pain will pass and life will bloom to unexpected discovery and delight.

Internal Work

Internal work with dreams is work I do almost every day. I work with men and women, young and old, some in the bud of life, some in the grip of death. I work with some in pain so bad that they can barely see. I work with some that have passed the point where even pain can reach. They all have one important thing in common. They work with dreams, and dreams bring about a better day.

I now do this work because I too have been into the pits. I help the bloody and the battered now because I myself was once within the ring of fire. This is what it means to be an analyst, to suffer and survive, and then to help other men and women as they pass through flame, transform themselves, endure the worst and overcome.

Some give this work a fancy name. It is sometimes called "psychoanalysis." Others refer to it as "analytical psychology." In more recent years, it has been called "psychoanalytic psychotherapy." I just call it analytic work. By any name, it is important work, perhaps the most important work that one can ever do.

In analytic work, analyst and client engage as equal partners to enter and explore the client's world within. No one is sick, no one is a patient. These are ordinary folk. The client is hurt; the analyst can help. And the analyst helps by decoding dreams.

Dreams are reflections of conditions in our internal world. They show us what is going on inside of us. This is where the work takes place. We cannot do much about the world outside, but we can change ourselves. And we work upon ourselves by means of work with dreams. Therefore, in the analytic hour, we talk about the present and the past, about feelings and the future, and then we dissect dreams.

The Language of Dreams

Every dream is a message, a telegram from our inner system up to us. Every dream brings us information that we need to know. In order that we live well and right according to our own original design, we and the inner apparatus must cohabit and cooperate. For this we must communicate. Dreams are that communication. Dreams forge the link between awareness and the life inside, a link that early on was natural, but was broken during childhood. Dreams repair the break. Dreams restore the system to its original integrity.

However, there is a problem. Dreams don't talk right. Dreams don't speak our native tongue. Dreams don't speak in abstract lukewarm words. Dreams speak instead a more powerful but archaic language. They speak in pictures and in stories. They speak in form of myth and legend. And they often are bizarre.

Understanding dreams is where the analyst can help. He or she translates dreams so that you can understand.

Where Dreams Come From

Dreams come from an inner kingdom which we find inside ourselves, an internal realm that always has existed but was hidden from our view. This inner kingdom is a world apart, a world that teems with unexpected life, with dinosaur and dog, with spirit and religion. Here we meet companions hitherto unknown. We watch them formulate our lives, sometimes on to fortune, sometimes to disaster. And here we find at last a chance for change and for new life. For having seen these things, we need no longer be a victim, a hapless captive crushed by unknown force. We can take our life in hand and fight to make it right.

The Way of Dreams

To work with dreams, we must accomplish four essential steps.

As the first step, we must get the dreams. This is simple to say, not so simple to do. We all dream, but some of us do not easily remember dreams. However, we all recall some dreams, and we can learn to recall more.

For good recall of dreams, we must first understand that they are valuable. We must realize that dreams are treasures which flow freely every night. They are like pieces of gold or small diamonds that come to us each time we sleep. They bring to us a priceless wisdom, for, by means of dreams, we gain knowledge of ourselves. If we grasp this fact, then we remember dreams.

Also in order to remember dreams, we must have sufficient sleep. Four or five hours of sleep is not enough. The natural human inclination is to sleep nine to ten hours every night. Seven or eight hours may be enough, but just barely. So we must allocate the night for sleep, or we will not have enough time with the life inside to make a difference.

Finally, if we are to recall dreams, we must protect our waking process. We should awaken slowly, a little at a time. Some things destroy dreams. Alarm clocks and telephones blast dreams away. If we jump up and race into the bathroom, dreams are gone. Instead, we need to awaken in a quiet place and turn our thoughts to dreams. We will find them still lingering in our memory, waiting there for us to come for them.

In trying to remember your own dreams, it helps to sleep alone. Otherwise, you may remember your partner's dreams. And if you sleep with someone else, you should instruct them never to awaken you from dreams. It is important that you finish dreams to find out how they end. The outcome of each dream is its most important part.

When we pay attention to our dreams, we can wake up a little in the night and memorize a dream, or we can write it down while half asleep. We need just enough attachment to the dream, a scrap or just one image, to pull it back when we awaken. And then it will all come up in one piece and in a rush.

As the second step to work with dreams, after we remember them, we must render them to concrete form. And we must do so right away. If we wake up and get up, the dream is gone for good. So we must attend to dreams the very first thing when we awaken in the morning. Right away on waking up we must write down dreams, or draw them up in pictures or in paintings, whichever is our inclination. This is an important process, for it forces dreams through pipelines of the mind, fixes them in language and in memory, colors and expands them, translates them from the evanescent into the absolute. Then we see the structure and dynamics of our own internal life. We see the starts and stops, progress, lapses, blunders, new horizons. We see our life enlarge and flourish as it begins the process to become what it always was designed to be. We see a life that is a marvel to behold.

When we have done this work, we wonder at how pale and tepid life used to be before. We wonder at how others manage to abide a world that, without dreams, seems so dreary and so gray. And we give thanks for our great good fortune that we have become acquainted with the life inside, and with our dreams.

As the third essential step of our internal work, we must learn to decipher dreams. We dismantle dreams. We extract the message from the medium. And then we find in dreams things that once we understood but had slipped away, and things we never knew. And over time with many dreams, we see the larger pattern of this life. We see direction and design in the weaving fabric of our own existence. We glimpse the core of who we are and can become.

And then we face the fourth and final step of work with dreams. The crucial step. We must respond. We must make a choice.

The Hard Part

As we have seen in Annie's case, this responding, this is the hard part. The Chance for Change brings along its fast companion, Necessity to Choose. No more the cry: *The devil made me do it!* We are now the one responsible. We are the architect in charge. And this is not so nice, as Annie's dreams do demonstrate. One great value in our life, one fundamental prime directive, is pit against another. Things we dearly do desire are mutually exclusive. And we must choose the one or choose the other.

This is where the rubber meets the road, here at the point of choice. Here we learn all too well that ignorance is surely bliss; that insight, while of value, exacts an awful toll. Each decision has a price. Each embrace of one thing excludes another. But no great advance ever comes without a cost, and there really is no other way. So we must make the painful choice, and the choice that we make must come from values.

Life at its cutting edge always does come down to this, the question of our values. Values are the central question of every human life. Which value will we choose, which value will we sacrifice? Which value will we follow, which value will we set aside?

Here at the point of choice no analyst can help us much. An analyst points out actions and reactions, but no analyst can ever tell you how to live. Your life is always yours to make or break by your own hand.

So in analytic work we find that we are on our own to play the game that has no rules, the game of life. Everything is up to us. We are untrained perhaps, and ill prepared, but all the same everything is up to us. To our ethics. To our honor. To the person we would hope to be. It is a hard responsibility, but we do have dreams to help us. Dreams rise out of us from our most authentic source. They tell us what is right for us in every circumstance. If we listen to our dreams, we will never go astray. Therefore, be not afraid. Dreams will tell you true. Dreams will free your mind.

And there is another fact we must consider. If we do not respond, if we fail to make the necessary choice, the choice is made for us. By default, the life inside will choose. This is not to be encouraged. The life inside surely is a treasure, but it has little tact. When it makes the choice, we often come away with blood upon our hands and with broken bones.

Unknown Outcome

Analytic work is not subject to prediction or control. It does not run a smooth or certain course or continue for a certain finite time. Dreams flow from an independent source that has its own agenda. Thus dreams bring to us whatever dreams will bring, whatever we then need. They hammer at us until we learn to cope, until we acquiesce to change. They have no mercy, they grant no easy passage. And the work is never well-defined, but is a moving target, open-ended and free ranging. We therefore cannot undertake to work with dreams with goals or preordained ideas, or with any ulterior motive. The analytic task requires more of us, most of all a purity of heart and courage in excess. And even then in every case the outcome is unknown. Therefore, our only hope is to go to work with dreams and follow where they lead. Here we can have some confidence. *You* can rely on *your* dreams. They arise inside of you. They are your own material; they are from your own internal life; they seek your best results. The more important question is on the other side: Can dreams rely on us?

We are the key. How and where the work will go, and with what speed, depends on us, upon our dedication and desire.

If we are honest and devoted, we will travel far and fast. Pain will pass and life will thrive. However, the reverse is also true. If we are coward or corrupt, if we shrink from stony choice, then we will languish in the scalding bog, as well we will deserve to do.

Examples of this last point abound in actual practice. When dreams insist on change, and change is not forthcoming, years of bitter discontent often follow. One wastes away, unhappy, yet unable or unwilling to make the choice that would make things better. Or worse yet, the life inside may tire of the struggle and bring things to an early and unseemly end.

A Winding Road

Like Annie, we all may sometime find ourselves upside down. We are then toxic to ourselves. In such a case, we need first of all to clear away existing structure, to tear apart old assumptions thus to find our bedrock. Until we do, we are infected and contagious. We are a danger to ourselves and to others all around. We are therefore by the life inside bombed and strafed and burned and broken up and put against the wall. Bad things happen in a rash because we have so much for which to answer. We must answer for the fact that we have too long ignored the most important aspect of ourselves, the inner center of our own existence. We have been arrogant and insolent. We must learn that the life inside is the master of our fate, that we are merely its exponent. We play our proper role only if we correctly carry out the life that lives within. If we do not, then early dreams lambaste us. The beginning part of analytic work can therefore be a desperate time.

But a desperate time will pass. It passes as we gain in understanding, as our attitudes begin to change. As we work with dreams, we begin to live a different way, and then our dreams take on a different task. They bring exciting new discoveries. They urge us on. We feel the cornerstone begin to shift. We find a new and better world in which to make our way. Dark clouds dissipate and we begin to see the better day.

New blood then flows into life. Everything warms up. Feelings once again emerge. And in the scarlet hue of new existence, dreams become companions. They comment on everything in life. They help us see around the corner. They have a clarity of vision not clouded by the selfish eye. They keep us straight inside ourselves, and this is wonderfully reflected in the life we live in our external world.

And there is something more, something wonderful. Dreams carry us beyond ourselves into the universe at large where we encounter spirit. We surrender to the spirit, coalesce therewith, and then return into this world with a new and better understanding of things supreme. It is here in the spiritual encounter that we find at last a sense of something sacred.

Unstructured Form

Just as the stuff of analytic work is all unstructured, so too the form thereof. The inner exploration follows no specific path or pattern. Subject to the principles of ethics and good practice, the work can take place once or twice a week or once or twice a month. It can be conducted while sitting in the sun or in the evening in a quiet room. It can be done sometimes by telephone, but is mostly face to face. It can last for months or last for years. The way of the work is never straight or short. It meanders all around. It goes here and there. It twists and turns and takes detours. But one thing always is the same. When the work has been well done, the inner exploration leaves its mark.

In every case of analytic work which is well and truly rendered, one's life is changed. Changed in ways altogether unexpected. Changed in ways that at the outset can never be foreseen. And, best of all, changed for the better in ways that will endure.

A Cost or a Call

When we begin the inner exploration, we may not lightly discontinue. We are, of course, free at any time to quit from work with dreams, and we should do so if not rewarded by results or when the analytic process naturally concludes. However, we must be aware that it is better not to go to work with dreams than it is to start and quickly stop. The life inside seeks participation in our lives. It will resent insincerity. If introduced and then rejected, it will likely take revenge.

We should also know that results from dreams may come not all at once, but may come in subtle ways and over time. But results will come, and come eventually with power. Images from dreams will radiate through life and burn themselves forever into memory. For years to come or for a lifetime, dreams will shine forth fresh and bright as beacons in the night by which to steer the better way. We will not again be lost in life. With dreams, we will always have our bearings.

Thus we will discover that dreams are letters from our inner friends. We then become inwardly attached, connected once again to the life inside. And we learn to decode dreams alone so that the inner exploration continues as a lifelong task, not as a chore, but as a second nature, and as a calling.

Spirit and Religion

When we follow dreams, we will find religion. Real religion as it was before the institutions cast dynamic life into sterile dogma. Religion that, when we are face to face with it, makes our hair stand up on end. This is religion for the stout of heart, for those who volunteer to undergo examination the same as Moses on the mountain, or as the Roman Saul upon the road to dark Damascus. In this encounter with real religion, we are baptized, tempted, tortured, dead, and resurrected, all in the mythic realm of dreams and lore. And this encounter has powerful effects.

This encounter with religion is where and how we learn to live of and for ourselves and for our people and our time. Where and how we learn to live according to our gifts and pursuant to our duty. Where and how we travel to the edge of our existence, engage the core of life itself, and return to pour ourselves in full into this daylight world into which so briefly we intrude.

The Undiscovered Country

The inner exploration is simple, yet profound. We work with dreams and they deliver up great gifts. They heal our wounds. They reveal the fundamental matters: our history, our destiny; the unseen reason for the fact that we are here. They slay the life already dead and lead us on to what is yet alive. They deliver us to spirit. Thus dreams are both challenge and salvation, trial by fire and rich reward.

With dreams, we find that we are not alone in life. Internal forces guide and guard us. We are invincible inside. The outside world may flail away in disarray. We may be buffeted and battered. But we are up to everything. We can be hurt but not destroyed. There is nothing that can for long impair our vigor. We are too engaged in life, making of it all that it can be. In fair or heavy weather, we are carried by an inner lucid calm, an abiding tranquil stillness at the center of the whole. No matter how wildly round the world may whirl, we are quiet and untroubled, steady and serene.

> For he or she among you
> that would have a miracle in your life,
> this is where and how you find it.

> In the undiscovered country,
> in the world inside yourself,
> hard at work with dreams.

◊   ◊   ◊   ◊

◊

◊   ◊

◊

4

DEFINITIONS

A GUIDE
FOR THE PERPLEXED

The dark side of the male —
war, revolution, rape, pillage

4

DEFINITIONS

The lyf so short,
the craft so long to lerne . . .

Chaucer

*A*LTHOUGH I HAVE ATTEMPTED to write this book without the magic words of academics in psychology, there are still herein concepts and ideas that are far from everyday experience. For that reason, with the kind advice of my editors, I have included here some definitions so as to be as plain as possible, and so that the ordinary reader might find in this part of the book some helpful explanations. The definitions that follow are not universal. Others may define things differently. But these are the definitions that I use, and they may help convey what it is I try to say.

The Human Psychological Apparatus

In addition to a physical anatomy, the human creature has also a psychic apparatus, a psychological anatomy. Just like the physical anatomy, it is subject to certain differences between men and women and to individual factors. Otherwise, this psychological anatomy is more or less the same for all of us. It is because of this that we can have a science of psychology, just as we have a science of anatomy, and that we can at least a little bit understand ourselves. This psychological system resides in the brain and the central nervous system, and it seems to encompass everything about us, our genetic history, our temperament, everything of which we are aware, and much more of which we are not aware. In other words, the human psychic system includes the whole brain-based structure, both the unconscious and the organ of awareness, which we call the ego complex, and it creates the peculiar and always intriguing psychology of the species, and of each of the individual creatures.

The Unconscious

The unconscious is our natural and unfiltered psychic life, the fundamental raw material for everything that follows. It is that part of the psychological apparatus that we know not of, over which we have no control, out of which all awareness grows. The unconscious is at all times a part of every individual human life. There is no way that we can escape from it or make it go away.

It contains all the many parts and pieces of ourselves. It is what I call the life inside.

At birth, the psychic apparatus and the unconscious are synonymous. When we are born, we have no awareness. We are only instinct, impulse, temperament, and emotion. Over time, and as a natural event, awareness rises out of the unconscious and accumulates so that, at about the age of twenty-five or thirty, each of us should have an adequate ego complex. But even then the unconscious continues to occupy the large majority of the total psychic system. It is a huge arena. It contains all the great initiatives of life, basic instinct, archetypal experience, and all the parts of personality which have not been assimilated into the ego complex.

The unconscious consists of various levels and layers. There is a personal unconscious which houses things we have done or learned and then forgot and also elements of unlived life. There is a family unconscious which contains the family gifts or the family curse. There is also a tribal unconscious, a clan unconscious, a national unconscious, a racial unconscious, and even a general human unconscious, each of which has positive elements and also a dark side. At the very deepest level, at the bedrock of the unconscious, we find equally powerful attractions to sexual exercise and

to spiritual experience. How we balance these two pre-
vailing predilections will determine the degree of our
development as individual men and women.

Awareness

Awareness is our conscious life which we perceive and
over which we have dominion and control. It is everything the brain retains that we have done or learned
and can direct, everything that is mentally accessible,
everything that is stored in memory or otherwise at
hand. It is our cognition of the world around us, our
capacity to think, compare, foresee, consider, and then
to make a choice. It has a certain detachment in that it
can see itself apart from what surrounds it. It stands
back, reflects, and then decides. It can even reflect
upon itself. The more we have of it, the better off we
are. Awareness is that peculiar faculty that sets apart the
human group.

The Ego Complex

The ego complex is not awareness in itself, but is the
organ or the structure of awareness. It is the organizing
apparatus of a complicated network of our genetic
gifts, our disposition, and our experience. It is fragile.
It can easily be damaged or impaired. If it becomes

defective, we have trouble coping with this life. We tend to make a mess of everything. But when the ego complex functions well, we can be quite remarkable. The ego complex measures and evaluates, makes judgments as to value and priority, makes and implements elaborate plans, confines impulse and emotion, and provides the framework for a life of vision and achievement. As compared to the vastness of the unconscious, the ego complex is small and feeble, puny even, and yet it is crucially important. It carries our one specific life in the context of our time. It is the only gateway into the external world for the expression of our native gifts. It is, in short, the crowning glory of the human species. But it must exist in service to the life inside or it becomes a toxin.

The Inner Rift (The Existential Problem)

As earlier observed, as adults we are split inside. This inner rift is the existential problem of human life. We are divided in ourselves and therefore seldom live at peace. There is no way we can avoid this division. It is inherent in our development. When in the natural course of life the ego complex forms and then matures, it pulls away from its host, the unconscious. This is a necessary step. In order to achieve free will and an independent life, the ego complex must establish a separate existence. But the process has an unexpected consequence. The ego complex is thereby isolated from the life inside. As a result, the ego complex becomes too proud and vain. It wanders off and goes astray. It entertains itself with frolics of its own. The outer and the inner parts of life no longer then communicate or cooperate. As a result, life turns dark and dangerous because we do not correctly represent the life inside.

We humans, we are a star-crossed lot. In our little lives, we must grapple with a mythic irony. In order to be truly free and to become aware, we must get some distance from the life inside. But that process is at once the source of misery and error. This is the problem of Eden. Remain ignorant and be comfortable, or become aware and also anxious. However, we have now the tools to solve the riddle. We know now that the step to an independent ego complex is only half the process. Once that has been accomplished, there is a second step that can occur. The ego complex can turn around and reconnect to the life inside. Then the inner split is healed and life flows smoothly once again as both sides perform their essential tasks in common purpose and in cooperation. But the work of reconnection is not well-known or widely understood, and it is not easy.

There are no manuals or guidebooks for this work. It is work we do asleep at night by means of dreams. It is the work we do in the analytic effort.

Analytic Work
In analytic work, we record and then decipher dreams in order to achieve the following four effects:

To heal our wounds.

To rebuild life according to original design, and to achieve the fully integrated personality.

To discover spirit.

To return into the waking world where now we function in a different way. Where in concert with our dreams we do the best we can with what we have while we are here. Where we do our duty to our people and our time. Where we body forth spirit and religion.

Animals and Instinct
Animals are frequent visitors in dreams. While we sleep, we see dogs and cats, horses, lions, tigers, all manner of the animal world. They usually represent instinctive life, the animal life of the body. We are all animals, mammals to be exact, and so we are subject to the animal instincts. These instincts are patterns of behavior which come as a part of the mammal package.

We are born with the instincts to eat, to sleep, to breathe, eliminate and copulate. When threatened, we fight or flee. But we are different from the animals in one important way. Animals are instinct pure and simple. They behave instinctively without thinking, as they must in order to survive. As a result, animals are always true unto themselves, for they can do only what is natural to them. Only humans, by our development of the ego complex, have free will, that is, the capacity to think and make decisions, to choose among competing values. And because we can so choose, we can choose to do things that are not natural to us, things that may actually be evil. Descartes was not far wrong when he said, *Cogito, ergo sum*. He failed to note, however, that the actual choices that we make yield all the difference in the quality of any given human life.

Archetypes

Archetypal images also frequent dreams. In contrast to the animals of instinct, archetypes are preexisting primal images in the minds of human beings. They are well-established patterns of behavior and ancient ideas. They are inherited and reside from birth inside each one of us. They show up in dreams and in movies, plays, books, or paintings, and sometimes in life itself in the external world. There are many examples. We all carry inside ourselves the image of the dying and the resurrecting god, the phoenix rising from the ashes of the fire. We all carry the idea of true love, of Lochinvar or of Tristan and Isolde. We all carry the mythic image of the hero, of Samson or of Lancelot. These are archetypal images which are inherent in the human creature. From time to time, an archetype may take possession of us and for a little while lift us up and out of this mundane world of practical affairs into the world of gods and glory. This is a powerful experience, but we cannot stay there very long. Necessity always calls us back into this world of nature and of instinct where we must do the animal things for our animal bodies. Thus we learn that there is not just one god that governs life, but two; one a god of sex and nature, the other a god of spirit and of power.

The Full Array of Inner Life

In dreams, you discover something quite surprising. You learn that the single individual is not a solitary unit, but that we are all made up of several parts and pieces. Besides the animals and archetypes, there are older men and women bearing wisdom, and there are children to signify the future. Of these inner figures,

there are four components parts which we see in
dreams most often. We see the ego complex, that is, we
see ourselves participating in our dreams. We see also
two companions of our same sex, both derivatives of
the ego complex. These are the ideal form and the dark
side. A man will have two masculine companions, a
woman two feminine companions. In addition, we are
accompanied by a companion of the other sex. These
four parts, the ego complex, two companions of the
same sex, and the contrasexual companion, plus the
core of life inside, make up the full array of our existence. Each part has its role to play. Each makes an
essential contribution to the whole.

The Ideal Form (also called "Persona")

The ideal form is our best foot forward, so to speak. As
we grow up, we learn that some parts of us are appreci-
ated whereas other parts are not. We tend to fasten to
the former and hide away the latter. Thus we create a
partial personality which includes all the better aspects
of ourselves, and excludes that which we find to be
incompatible. We send this form out into the world to
make our way therein. This appears to others to be the
person that is you or me. But this form is not the
whole of us, and it leaves much of us unconsidered.

The Dark Side (the Shadow)

When we create the ideal form, the other and un-wanted aspects of ourselves do not just go away. We may choose not to lie or cheat, but we still have these possibilities inside of us. So we put these unwanted pieces into exile, not knowing that they will still exact a price in life. Eventually we see these forms again, either outside in the world because they have escaped, or in our dreams. We will be shocked someday to find inside ourselves a dark, degenerate, evil twin. A woman will be appalled to learn that she is full of intrigue and treachery. A man will be dismayed to find inside himself a savage who does rape and murder for amusement. These dark partners are the other side of who and what we are and have been taught to be. And the most frustrating piece of this enigma is that we cannot make these dark forms do better or even keep them in control. They run around wherever we may go doing harm to others.

But there is a way that we can stop the carnage. The ideal form and the dark side are both reflections of the ego complex. They are linked together as images in a mirror. As we make the ideal form more extravagant, so the shadow side is more depraved. Likewise, as the ideal form becomes less perfect, so the shadow is less dark and evil. Therefore, as somewhat of a surprise, we find that in order to be less dark and evil, we must be less nice. We must dissolve as far as possible the ideal form so that it is not so pure and flawless. The dark side then naturally is less corrupt, and will stay with us instead of running off to injure others. We may then discover that this dark side is an interesting companion. It has a dry ironic sense of humor, and it is always seeking our best interests, but in unusual and devious ways. It is creative and also ruthless. In case of danger, it will fight for us, and when all the worst has come to us, this dark comrade will still be there to pick us up and find a way out of the rubble.

The Contrasexual Companion

As observed above, in addition to the ideal form and the dark side, we find in dreams a companion of the other sex. A woman will find in dreams the image of a man or many men, whom we call the animus. A man will find in dreams the image of a woman, whom we call the anima. He or she is a figure of great power, the animating force of life, who is also sometimes full of animosity. This is the image of the contrasexual soul, not the soul as in theology, but the soul as in psychology, the archetype of meaning and of purpose.

The contrasexual companion can be problematic. The animus, in his raw and natural state, is dangerous. He tries to dominate the woman, to carry her away. He seeks to wreck and ruin her so that he will live while she will languish. And all too often, the woman is a willing victim. In contrast, the anima in her natural state is retiring and receptive. She waits for the man to worship her, and, if he does not (and he seldom will), then she turns to acid, and she will poison and corrode his life in ways too subtle and too painful even to imagine. The ordinary woman must fight her masculine companion thereby to win respect, whereas the man must bow down to the greater wisdom of his feminine companion. These figures then become our allies.

The contrasexual soul has two assignments in this life. In youth, it functions for biology. Without our knowledge or consent, she or he sneaks out into the outside world, there to find and captivate a mate for us. It works this way. The contrasexual soul projects itself into the outside world, finds a suitable person of the other sex, and wraps itself around that other person. Then, when we look out and see that other person, we see our own internal soul. Well, this is pretty heady stuff. We are just bowled over. We go a little mad. With our soul so close at hand, we must have it. The urge to union is thoroughly compelling. Passion flares, and marriage and maybe children follow in some order. Unfortunately, these events have nothing at all to do with happiness. They have only to do with the basic requirement of life that we reproduce the species.

The second task of the contrasexual soul arrives at the middle point of life. Here the soul must be repatriated, must be brought back home to our internal world. This is because the soul has unique features. The soul is the only figure in the psychic apparatus that moves freely back and forth between the inner world and the ego complex. In doing so, the contrasexual companion carries messages between the life inside and our awareness, and so brings about a better understanding between the two. Thus the animus or anima builds a bridge between the organ of awareness and the core of life inside. We thereby regain that union which was lost when we first became aware. And more. When the masculine soul comes home into the ordinary woman, he will bring to her his courage and his vision, and he will be a better friend to her than any man who lives and breathes and moves across this plain of pain and loss and fixed limitation. In a similar way, when a man unites with his internal feminine companion, she will bring to him an understanding and compassion and capacity for love that he will never ever otherwise possess. And she will be for him a more exquisite intimate acquaintance, more loving and more faithful, than any woman who ever walks this earth in mortal form or makes a promise that she cannot keep. This inner union has remarkable effects. When either man or woman is reconnected through the anima or animus to the core of life inside, then he or she will once again discover and become who and what they really are and always were designed to be.

The Inner Center

There is formed at our conception a core of our unique existence. It resides at the center of the psychic apparatus. It is sometimes called the self. By whatever name, it is the acorn out of which will grow every limb and leaf of the tree of life to follow. This inner center is the home of our original design, our natural proclivity. It contains also, coded directly into the central nervous system, all of the experience of every ancestor in our line. This is a very large number. In 500 years, it is about one million men and women. In 2,000 years, it is the number one followed by twenty-four zeroes, a trillion trillion. In other words, we each carry inside ourselves all the experience of the human condition.

This vast array of knowledge is called the collective unconscious, and it may appear to us in dreams as the Wise Old Man or Woman who has done everything and knows everything. The inner center sometimes itself appears in dreams, but in the image of the President or as the King or Queen. Other than in dreams, this inner core of life is not directly seen or heard. Yet, throughout life, it exerts a gentle pressure that steers us toward the path that we have been by it prepared to trod. This core of life is ever present. It is the quiet voice you hear at night. It is your natural disposition and your character. It includes elements of fate. It points always to the future. And it demands of you the best of you, all the time every day in every way.

Spirit and Religion

When we go into the world inside ourselves and to the central core thereof, we find something special waiting for us there. We find a gateway to the world beyond. A world beyond this world, a world beyond ourselves, the world of spirit and religion. If we are brave enough and strong, we pass through this gate and for a little while sail out into that new dimension, into the universe at large, where we confront powers greater than ourselves, all manner of great gods and goddesses who carry fate and create destiny. Here with them we find at last an absolute religion, religion in its pure and perfect form, religion as an attitude of reverence and of wonder, religion without rules or doctrine. Here we encounter spirit, the living energy of whatever is divine, the fire of god that burns and yet does not consume. If we are brave enough, we breathe this fire into ourselves and so become a vessel of the holy ghost, a part and parcel of the universal life. We then return into this rough external world to carry forth unto our people and our time the fire and flame of spiritual renewal.

This is what it means
to be religious.

To carry forth the fire of god
within the heart.

◊   ◊   ◊   ◊

◇

◇   ◇

◇

5

ANNIE'S STORY — SECOND YEAR

THE
RETURNING

The oppressive animus

5

ANNIE'S STORY — SECOND YEAR

To strive, to seek, to find,
and not to yield.

Tennyson

*A*NNIE SURVIVED THE ATTACK by the dark side of life and grew stronger and more dedicated. As a result, the analytic work took up a new direction. Criticism became encouragement. Reproach became acclaim. In her second year of analytic work, Annie turned the corner. Of course, the path was neither smooth nor all downhill, but the way was cleared at last for the contemplation of the finer aspects of Annie's life. And this new life, with all its ups and downs, with all its promise and potential, was carried forth in Annie's dreams.

January 8th — Animals
  I have come home for a family visit. There are some animals in the house. Two polar bears are upstairs, and there is a gorilla in the yard. I know that one of the polar

bears is in my room tearing it apart. I'm trying to get its attention by saying, "Here kitty, kitty." But it doesn't pay any attention. Eventually I stumble onto its name and it begins to listen to me and to do a little bit of what I ask. I make it go outside. The gorilla is out there climbing in the trees. The bears and the gorilla don't hurt me, but I know I don't have much control over them, and that I am in a dangerous situation.

Annie here contends with the animals of her inner life, animals that were born at home. The bears and the gorilla, these are elements of instinct. Such elements are a part of all of us, the animal base for life itself. They are the forms of our biological existence. They can be dangerous, but they are not always harmful. And they are essential, for the spirit of our existence rides upon our animal inheritance. But animals make demands. We are like any other animal; we must eat, eliminate, play, sleep, reproduce. This instinctive life is powerful, like bears or a gorilla. It can sometimes run away with us, as it has in the past run away with Annie. But Annie now has gained some ground. She is able to avoid direct assault. And she has learned to talk to the animals. This is quite significant. Because Annie can now communicate, she can control the bears a little bit, at least enough to avoid an injury. Annie can with care maintain her safety from instinctive overload. She has gained the upper hand. She is no longer just a victim. She is now at least the equal of her own instinctive nature. This really is a great advance.

Love in Two Acts
October 2nd — Love: Act One

My sister and I are on a special ride. She's been on it before, but I have not. The ride begins with scenes of everyday life such as families playing in the yard or children going off to school. Then my sister says, "Get ready. Here comes the good part." Suddenly we plunge over a black edge into darkness. We are no longer moving on a linear plane. Our bodies are floating and swirling among the planets and among particles of pretty red dust. It is all so beautiful and thrilling. Then we land on a musical table in a room full of games. The table is sectioned off in many different colors. Each section is numbered and makes a different sound. My sister and I dance on the top of the table. We make music with our feet by jumping from place to place. This is really great! All the sections are angular in shape, but there is one big section in the center that is round. I jump on it, and it goes "Bang" and makes the sound of a cymbal.

After exposing the problem with sex, dreams undertook to educate Annie, to show her that something else and something better may lie within her grasp. Outside the family circle, Annie had no direct experience of having loved another. But, as explained in the preceding chapter of definitions, Annie carries inside herself all the experience of her ancestors, and many of them have loved and been loved. So an inner sister comes to show Annie what she had so far missed, to initiate Annie into the mystery of love as opposed to unrelated sex. In the dream, this inner sister takes Annie to that special ride on which Annie has not been before, the special experience of love.

As the dream reflects, everything begins within the framework of an ordinary family life. Then suddenly, something unexpected happens and we plunge over the edge of ordinary life and out into the dark unknown. We no longer move in lineal form, but float among the stars in a swirl of haze and passion, in a red fog of feeling and emotion. One is lost in the incandescent glow of something wonderful. One becomes an instrument of rhapsody and ecstasy. So we see that Annie in this dream becomes acquainted with the age-old and universal experience of love; love at its very best, love as the beauty and the music of this life.

Annie is among the lucky ones. Not everyone while on this earth encounters love. We therefore can conclude that Annie is being prepared by this dream for something really special up ahead.

January 25th — Love: Act Two
Dr. Hagan is talking to me about love. He paces as he speaks. Then he stops and looks right at me and our eyes meet and lock and get really big. I'm totally focused on exactly what he's saying. He knows that I'm taking it all in and that I'm absorbing everything he's telling me.

Annie has met a young man. He is a nice young man. He likes her and she likes him. So naturally, she is much interested in this thing called love. Because Annie is uneducated in matters of the heart, she needs to learn about love, as much as possible as quickly as possible. So the life inside responds and sends up to Annie dreams of love. Therefore in analytic work, love becomes a matter of discussion. Annie concentrates on this discussion. She is keenly focused. And thus she learns that love is the great redemption and reward for this hard life so full of demand and discontent.

Be not afraid, for there is also love within this world.

Love, the great force which carries life and moves mountains, and moves also men and women. Love, the saving grace, the unmatched compensation for our hard labor in this harsh and unforgiving land.

Annie is now able to grasp this new knowledge of the power and the majesty of love. She begins to see how love may enter in and enrich her own life. She begins to feel the finer possibilities for her own future. She begins to look forward with hope and expectation.

February 12th — Earthquake

I am at work in a tall building. I go to the window and notice a very dark cloud overhead. Then suddenly a massive earthquake strikes. I run and get under my desk. The building shakes wildly back and forth and I can see through my window that it is swinging from side to side almost to the ground. I know I won't survive. I'm sure I'm going to die. But then the earthquake stops. I get up and look around. The office is a mess. I ask the others if they are all right, and they are. We look for a way out. We find a stairwell which leads down to the street. I pick up my belongings and we all walk down the stairs. As we reach an exit, I ask a woman if the building has collapsed. She tells me no, our building is okay. It is strong and sturdy and, no matter what, it never will fall down. We go out on to the sidewalk and I am shocked by what I see. There are lots of injured people in the street. I realize that, since I am one of the survivors, I have to help the others, and I begin to do so.

An earthquake in a dream reflects a great change in life. The earth has actually moved under our feet. So Annie has been subjected here to a massive change in attitude and in her prospects. This is evident in the metaphoric declaration that Annie's building, the structure of her life, is no longer weak and puny like the tiny wall in the dream of heavy weather. Annie's life has been reconstructed. Her structure is now large and strong and flexible. It bends, but does not break. And she is told that it is now so strong that it will never come apart.

What a change! When Annie first began this work, she had nothing to protect her from the hardships of this life. But now, after inner exploration, Annie finds herself within an unbreakable structure.

This is absolutely work well done.

In addition, and of great significance, Annie now begins to grasp a sense of purpose for her own existence. She sees that others are hurt and she can help. She sees that she can make a difference. She understands that, as one who has survived, she has a duty now to offer up herself into the world to impart aid to others who are themselves besieged and brought low by broken bones and broken hearts.

February 17th — Invasion and Redemption

   I'm on a small island off the coast of Greece. All of a sudden there are several large explosions on the mainland. The entire mainland is completely destroyed. There is no life anywhere. I know they're going to hit my island next. All the island inhabitants gather together. Each person prays to a wooden plaque that he or she has made. Mine has a Chinese symbol on it that looks like the symbol for Yin and Yang. It has two words inscribed on it, one of which is "Come." Then two Darth Vaders arrive on the island with all their forces. The others and I run for cover. I find a place to hide, but it's too small for me. Then I'm on the open sand and grenades are landing all around me. I run, but everywhere I go there's another volley of grenades. I can't find safety anywhere. Soldiers come and start killing people. They shoot at me, but miss. I pretend that I've been hit and lie on the ground as if I'm dead. But I'm so scared that my body shakes. Some of the soldiers run past me thinking that I'm dead, but two others notice that I'm moving. They stop. One tells the other that he's going to put one more bullet in me to make sure that I am dead. But I get up and run away before he has time to shoot. I have a handgun now, and I'm running for the border to get away. I'm getting close. I think I'm going to make it. But then I run into a patrol full of soldiers armed with rifles. Many others have made it to the border, too, but now we're all surrounded by this patrol. They are about to shoot the lot of us, but a girl soldier hesitates. Another soldier says, "What are we waiting for? Kill them all!" But the girl soldier says, "No, we're going to give them one last chance." They argue loudly, but she prevails. Then the soldiers give us one small mattress each. They say that this is all we get. They tell us this is all that's left, that everything else has been destroyed, that we must do the best we can with what we have. We must rebuild by ourselves. I kneel down on my mattress and I begin to cry. I can't believe that I am going to live. I am completely drained, but so very thankful that my life was spared. Then, from far away, I hear the sound of music, a beautiful song, a song about love and second chances.

Wow!

What a dream! It takes your breath away. A dream like this requires little explanation. Everything is in the feelings. Feelings that for Annie were utterly intense.

This dream is the story of Annie's life.

Annie was put down for death, but was spared.

Annie was to be undone, but she endured.

Evil forces came to kill her, but she survived, and in the effort got a second chance, a second chance at life, a chance for love.

A dream like this is a religious experience. It is, indeed, Amazing Grace, the words of which so eloquently describe Annie's actual experience.

> Amazing grace, how sweet the sound,
> that saved a wretch like me,
> I once was lost, but now am found,
> was blind, but now I see.

Annie started out in life without reverence, without piety. In the family home, everything was material and conventional. No one taught the spiritual values. So Annie had to learn somehow herself. And she is learning here by means of dreams.

This dream begins at the cradle of Western civilization, in Greece, the site of the golden age of excellence and purity. It is our Garden of Eden. But this Garden is invaded by powerful and evil elements which have turned the force of life to darker purpose. So Annie turns to prayer. She prays to a religious relic that she has fashioned for herself, one which calls her to her destiny. But she finds that prayer is not enough. In dreams, action counts. If one will not act, the renegades run wild. And in her dream, Annie's world becomes a killing ground. The carnage is truly terrible. Annie is afraid. She tries to hide, but hiding will not work. One must fight. Finally, exhausted and without hope, Annie is cornered and captured. She comes face to face with her own destruction. But, in a surprising finish to the dream, because of her new found sense of reverence and respect, Annie is given a new start, a clean slate, another chance. Annie is here granted what we might call redemption.

The price of this redemption has been severe. Nothing much is left of Annie's former life. It has been almost wiped away. She must now rebuild from plain bare ground. But she is at least alive. And she has one tool, a mattress, a place where she can sleep, a place where she can dream. And dreams will see her through.

Then, from somewhere far far away, Annie hears music, a beautiful melody of love, a song of second chances. Annie is spent, she is exhausted, but she is full of gratitude and hope, for she has received a very great gift, the gift of life, and also now the gift of love.

May 10th — The Swing

I'm in the front yard of the family home. I am up a tree and sexually aroused. Others in my family are playing in a hot tub down below. I feel sad because I have to leave and go back to my own home. Then I'm on a rope swing connected to a tree branch. I'm swinging really high, back and forth. My sister yells at me to be careful. The branch is about to break. I am afraid that I will fall, and I yell to her to stop me because I cannot stop myself. She reaches out for me but misses on the first two tries. Then she finally catches hold of me and lands me safely.

This is a sharp setback for Annie. This dream shows her failure to step up to the second chance that she received, and reflects the worst condition that one can have in dreams. Swinging wildly back and forth is a dire situation. One has no center, no ballast. One is unstable, one flies without pause from one extreme to another. This swinging reflects Annie's indecision. Annie is still a reluctant heroine, still loath to let go of her family and her past in order to move into her future, and this makes her still at risk. In this dream, she has lost control again. If some inner figure does not come to Annie's aid, because of her reluctance, Annie may crash and do herself another dose of serious harm.

This condition is the direct result of Annie's regressive longing for the family. And, for whatever reason, the dream expressly ties the family to Annie's sexual self-indulgence. We do not know why the dream makes this connection, but that is not the salient point. Dreams tells us facts. Reasons are irrelevant. With or without an explanation, we must respond to facts.

Annie's regressive longing is not the problem of the family. This is Annie's inner flaw. She still cannot let go, she still desires the warmth and comfort of the family group. So she finds herself first up a tree and then aboard a wild and reckless swing.

This family matter is a real problem for Annie. She longs to remain enclosed within the family system. But this creates a quandary. Sometimes a family structure does not permit a child to have an individual life. Sometimes the two are mutually exclusive. This puts the child in an untenable position. In such a case, he or she must choose the one and sacrifice the other. The question is, which will he or she select, which will he or she refuse? For the child involved, there really is no question.

We must always choose our own existence. We can never choose to live by or for another, no matter who he or she may be.

This is what Siddhartha learned from the Buddha. The one essential thing in life is to be true unto our own original design, to our individual destiny. If we choose to serve another, other than our child while he or she is young, such a choice will result in rot, in our own decay. This is sacrilege. The life inside will soon or late explode in indignation.

Obligations in this life run downhill, from one generation to the next. Nature does not run backwards to the past. Nature runs forward to the future. We are always obligated to fulfill our own life and then protect our children. Except that we should do no harm to others, we owe nothing to an older generation. We owe nothing to churches, or to schools, or to convention. We owe everything to the future and to the person that we were born to be.

Everywhere we turn in life, there is always a friend or a lover or a parent, or all of them, making claim on us. Unless we sometimes render them unhappy by refusing to comply, we are not caring for ourselves enough, and we will surely suffer consequences. It is our duty to live well and right according to our own internal life, not according to ideas of others. We must at all costs stay out of Procrustean beds. We must find and keep our feet upon the road that is right for us.

Others must adjust themselves so that we are free to be the person of our destiny. If others really love us, this is not a problem. But if they just *want* something from us, then we are merely lunch.

It is never right to sacrifice ourselves to make someone else happy, or in an effort to keep someone by our side. It will never work. We just lose them and in the bargain also lose our self-respect. Those who are meant to be with us come freely of their own accord. Those who are not meant to be with us will wander off and no power on this earth can hold them back. If we try, we will just succeed to wreck ourselves. So here we really have no option. We can only live the life we have as best we can, and let others come and go as they are wont to do.

There is another important point about this dream. It is an example of what will happen when we refuse to make the hard decision. In that case, we lend ourselves to self-destruction. In the dream, divided loyalties have unhinged Annie. Although she knows that she must leave, she cannot bring herself to do so. This is the cost of being too congenial, the price of approval and acceptance. And it robs Annie of her individual advance. Annie therefore oscillates between extremes. Unless this wild swinging back and forth is somehow interrupted, some terrible event will take place actually in life to dictate a decision. You see, it is like this: If we will not make the hard decision, the inner system makes it for us. But the inner apparatus is not so gentle. It makes decisions with a spray of blood and broken bone. Better to grit our teeth and decide ourselves. Otherwise, everything we value may be lost, for when fed up, the life inside simply destroys everything. It does not make the fine distinctions. It just brings down the house, thus forcing us to start again. Accordingly, this dream depicts another point of peril for Annie, another point of progress or of failure.

Sooner or later, Annie will herself have to choose to sacrifice her interest in the family, or she will reap the bitter harvest of her own inaction. She will lose the second chance at life she worked so hard to win. But here Annie is lucky once again. As in the past, an inner sister comes to Annie's aid. She warns Annie of the danger and, when Annie cannot help herself, her sister reaches out and stops the wild rotation.

August 17th — The Chasm

I am in a desert area where strange giant furry shrimp live at the bottom of a gorge. One or two other people are with me. I am curious about the giant shrimp, and I start climbing down the cliff to get a better look. All of a sudden, sand and rocks give way in an avalanche. The shrimp below are covered up and smothered. I suddenly realize that I am in a very dangerous place. This cliff is unstable and treacherous. I need to get back up as quickly as I can, or I'll fall and end up smothered too. But I find I cannot go back. I can only go forward. So I begin to move cautiously around the gorge and across the chasm. I take great care to step only on hard rock so I don't lose my footing and go tumbling down. I test each rock before I place my full weight on it. In this way, I slowly climb across the chasm and up the other side. Finally, completely exhausted, I lift myself over the edge and onto the solid ground of the other side. I have crossed over.

Annie is back on the road. Her dream has brought her here to explore the depths of her own internal world. And she is no longer alone; she travels now with inner friends. Annie seeks here to examine strange creatures that dwell deep inside herself. But she is still unsteady, and she is on treacherous ground. The footing is unsure and dangerous. She starts an avalanche and does some damage to the creatures she has come to see. She retreats, but finds she cannot go back. She must go forward, she must cross the chasm. That is, she must make a major change in her inner attitudes. She must resolve the conflict that paralyzes her, the conflict between her own real nature and what others ask of her. She cannot return to the way things were. She must advance to a new standpoint. But she must do so carefully. One false step could cast her down into the void and smother her in dirt, debris, and rubble.

Annie has been altogether too agreeable in this life. She has always done what others have demanded of her. This has hurt her, and it condemned her companions of the inner world to live in poverty and neglect. Annie must now change her ways. This dream tells her how to do so. By being very careful, by moving forward very slowly but with resolution, and by making certain that she is on a solid footing at every step along the way, Annie can cross over.

This is a teaching dream, a dream of instruction. It shows Annie how she can change her life. It shows us how we can change our lives. We change our lives one step at a time, each step on solid rock. If we can take just one more step, we can get through anything! And Annie does so here. She succeeds! And so this dream tells Annie that she can succeed in her external world. She can cross over. She can separate herself from family and so realize her individual life.

September 8th — The Mother's Monster

I am at my mother's house. I see outside a creature, a huge animal, that has the legs of a horse and the body of a giant crab. It can walk on either two legs or four, or it can slither along the ground as if it has no legs at all. The creature comes up to the house and unlocks the door to my mother's room with its own key. It goes in and turns on the stereo with its giant crablike claws. I am amazed and frightened. I try to tell my mom about this thing, that it unlocked her door and went into her room. But I can't get through to her. She just doesn't understand. I'm getting to a point of panic. I see the creature return to a pasture next to the house. Then several small but strong and fast crocodiles come crawling up out of some water and into the house. My brother shows up and helps me fight them off. I have one by the mouth, which I clamp closed with my hands. I'm afraid to let go because it's trying to bite me. I kick other crocodiles back into the water. All the time, I have the strong feeling that I'm supposed to be leaving.

This is a dream showing Annie once again the dangers of her family home. Annie can now see more clearly the problems dwelling there. Her mother harbors a strange monster, part horse, part crab, and crocodiles are still a fixture.

The horse/crab creature has the keys to Annie's mother's life. He freely comes and goes. He controls her feelings, the music in the dream.

Annie's mother is still oblivious to the creature's coexistence. Annie tries to tell her, but she does not listen. No matter what Annie says to her, she does not see this reflection of her inner life. However, the situation has improved a little. The horse/crab creature is calm, and the crocodiles are smaller, although still quick and mean.

Annie is also now more brave and strong, and she has help from an inner brother. She is better able to defend herself, to fight the dangerous creatures of the family home that continue to attack. And she sees again that she cannot remain at home.

Annie can no longer just ignore the directive from the life inside that she separate from her family. But will she really do it? Does she really have the dark resolve to do the uncongenial? We do not yet know. We can only wait and see.

September 10th — The Lightning Storm

I am at a house by a lake with my sister and my mother. I look out and see a huge explosion across the lake, a series of explosions. They ignite one house after another in swift succession as they come around the lake. It is a series of electrical explosions, lightning strikes, a lightning storm. The lightning storm is making its way around the lake, heading for us. I know it's going to hit us soon and that when it gets here the current will be even stronger. I see streaks of white lightning flying through the sky, and I yell for everyone to find a place in the middle of the room away from any electricity. My mom, my sister, and I all huddle together. I'm afraid the lightning will destroy my capacity to have children. I'm using my mom and my sister as a shield. I also grab a coat to put over me. I lay on my stomach so that the current will hit my back and hopefully not damage my reproductive organs. The lightning hits. My sister screams. I feel the lightning hit my back. The pain is excruciating, unbearable. The current continues for a long time. It seems like forever, but finally it moves on. After the storm has passed, I am dazed and weak, but still I manage to sit up. I see that water from the lake has risen all the way to the foundation of the house. I know the storm is on a circular path and that it is just a matter of time before it comes around and hits our house again. It gains strength with each revolution so that the next time will be even worse. I wonder if the next time the storm will cause the lake to rise and flood the house completely. I wonder if we can survive the next time.

This dream is really scary. It threatens Annie's children.

It is still uncertain what Annie will choose to do about the family hold on her. She has been unable yet to make the dark decision. She cannot yet accept the sacrifice to sever family ties. So she has done nothing.

But now the life inside has had enough. The inner system throws down the gauntlet. It draws a line. The life inside here shows Annie what her lack of courage is going to cost. If she will not make the change, then she will lose her children.

There! Is that enough? Will that get her attention? I can tell you, Annie was horrified at the implications of this dream.

This dream told Annie clearly that, if she does not gain some distance from her family, not only will her own life end in ruin, but the family toxin will flow through her and lay claim upon her children.

Now what will Annie do?

If she will not do the right thing for herself, will she do the right thing for her children? Will she gather up her nerve and break the ties that bind?

If this dream won't move Annie into action, then nothing will, for there is no greater force in human life than a mother's instinct to protect her children.

October 5th — The Blue Jewel

My sister and I are on top of a snow-covered hill. A giant clear blue jewel breaks free from the snow and ice and rolls down to the bottom of the hill. My sister shouts and runs after it. She runs a long way to catch up with it. The jewel collects snow as it rolls. When it finally stops at the bottom of the hill, it is completely covered with layers of snow and ice. When my sister finally catches up with the stone, she wants to get inside the snowball so she can see the jewel. But I tell her she's too little, that she does not have the strength to break through all that snow and ice. But she begins to try.

The threat to Annie's children finally did it. She has chosen. And she chose to save her children. So she is extracting herself from the family web. Inch by painful inch, she is withdrawing from family demands. She is establishing some boundaries. Others are quite unhappy. But the inner life is overjoyed. And this dream is Annie's reward, this wonderful discovery.

Annie's spiritual life has been delivered to her in this blue jewel of her dream.

Annie's sacrifice of family made all the difference. It broke the logjam. It set a new direction for her work. Everything that happens now is possible because the sacrifice was made. Such a sacrifice is difficult. But the rewards are also great. Life is lost without the sacrifice. Life is won when the sacrifice is made. The sacrifice itself is the gateway to the future. In this case, Annie's sacrifice has led directly to the gift of spiritual awareness, which forms the next step of the analytic work.

The beautiful blue jewel contains Annie's inner spirit. Its discovery marks a magic moment in her internal exploration. This fine blue stone is the repository of all of Annie's gifts, her future possibilities, her destiny. It has been buried all her life, but now has broken free. It carries all that Annie is or may become, and all of Annie's intangible existence.

But Annie has a problem.

The stone is covered over with crusted snow and ice, and Annie is not moved to clear it off. Annie still thinks too little of herself. She cannot yet fathom that she is herself this rare wonder. She feels too small and weak to strip and polish this great treasure. In contrast, her sister is eager to expose the jewel, to chip away the frozen casing and lay bare the luster of the stone.

Annie must reassess herself. She must step up to her better possibilities. She really does possess the power to uncover and to burnish this blue jewel. It will be a long and arduous undertaking, but well worth the effort. This is the cornerstone of Annie's life. Everything of Annie's years to come will roll out of this fine stone. But Annie walks away.

Annie's apathy seems incomprehensible, but it is a frequent problem of the inner exploration, the most perplexing part of analytic work. We shy away from greatness. Everyone readily admits that he or she is inadequate or evil. We are trained from early on to accept the worst about ourselves. But we are reluctant to embrace the best.

We cannot believe that we have any special aptitude, a mission, or a reason to exist. We shrink from virtue. We seek only to belong. The community is comforting. We are slow to leave the warmth of being in the herd. Therefore, when in a dream we see a special treasure, we are prone to close our eyes and walk away. We do not wish to grasp that we are cut above the crowd. It is too improbable. And worse, if true, we might then have responsibility. We might no longer drift through life at ease, lazy to the last. We might then, God forbid, have special qualities which give rise to special duties. Better to remain among the great unwashed average of the mob. Better to have no recognition and no special gifts. But in analytic work, one may not hide or run away. Like it or not, special qualities will out. Analytic work finds the special gift and exacts the special duty, which one may not refuse.

This is the Moses problem. When God called Moses into Egypt to free the people, Moses politely did decline. Moses offered only this: "Please, God, send my brother, Aaron. He is much more fit for such a task." (Aaron, of course, was not there to urge on God to Moses.) But there on hallowed ground upon the mountaintop, God examined Moses, and the will of God prevailed.

God prevails! Destiny prevails! But Annie hesitates. Annie's sister, though, is keen to clean the stone. She knows that this blue jewel will enrich Annie's life beyond excessive expectation. She knows that purpose and direction and rare knowledge of the spirit wait for Annie in this stone. She knows that this fine stone is yet the source and origin of all that Annie is and will become. And someday, too, Annie will realize the wonder of this gift, and appreciate her fate.

March 3rd — Treasure Island
A religious man walks along a series of paths that branch out in different directions. He is deep in thought and talks to himself as he walks along. I am with two others and tell them to follow me as I walk behind him

with my hands folded in prayer. I tell them that he is the messiah. He is also my beloved, but he is not pleased with us because he wants to be alone just now to contemplate religion. So I break away and branch out on my own. My friends and I walk to a dock at the edge of a bay of water. I sit down in an old wooden chair, but the chair flips over and I fall into the water. It is not dangerous or deep, in fact, it is quite nice. I have a feeling that there's something special out there in the water waiting for me. I call for the others to come with me, and we swim out to see what might be there. We find a current where the water is warm and clear. Then we see an island where springs spout up amid lush green foliage. It is very beautiful. We swim to the island and go ashore. I pick a handful of leaves from a bright green plant. They sparkle in my hand and each has a different pattern just like snowflakes do. I can't believe how lovely these leaves are.

This is a wonderful dream. It carries Annie to her religious bedrock and to her individual existence.

At the beginning of the dream, Annie is in the midst of her full personality, the four of them as explained in the Definitions. The women follow the masculine figure who is intent upon the varieties of religious experience. Annie is interested in him, but she is also now quite different, not so willing any more simply to conform. She has grown wiser and stronger. She has gained a sense of herself, she has ideas of her own. So she does something daring. She leaves the man to seek her own way, the feminine way. This simple act is of immense importance. By this one deed, Annie becomes responsible at last.

We have rarely seen Annie make decisions in these dreams. She has often needed help. She has rarely exercised discretion. However, Annie here strikes out on her own, as a leader of her inner friends.

This is exactly what was needed. Annie is proving worthy of her trial. A new awareness has been created. New possibilities abound.

This is what everything has been about. Annie has been rebuilt, and now she holds the future in her hands. According to the dream, Annie's new direction takes her to the water's edge. By another piece of luck, she falls in. She finds that this is not so bad, for it is the stream of life, now flowing clear and warm. Annie senses that something special waits for her, something of surpassing value. With her companions at her side, and braver now, Annie goes to find whatever there is calling her. And here she finds her promised land, her individual island in the stream, bursting with new and verdant life, free-flowing springs, and plants of rare and stunning beauty. Annie here has found her future life, the source of who and what she will become.

This treasure island is Annie's individual existence, a place of natural and organic growth. Annie is astonished by the profound grace and goodness of it all. And so she should be. When she began her analytic work, there was no way to predict that it would lead to this result. Things in life were bad, and might have gotten worse. In undertaking to do the inner exploration, she made a brave choice. Annie chose to fight for life. She chose not to let heartbreak and mishap wreck and ruin her. She chose not to follow in the paths of conventional religion or the general average avenues of quiet desperation. She chose to pursue her promise and potential in an individual life, a life far different from the family life before. As a result, Annie is no longer trapped and captured in a floating foreign prison, a Devil's Island of the mind. She has fought and won her freedom and did thereby reclaim her future.

Annie is now in charge of life, at least to some extent. She does not stand idly by while events swirl madly past. She reaches out to participate, to find her best potential; to find her finest incarnation. She may now become who and what she really is and always was designed to be. She may find at last and live the life that is and always was her natural estate.

Annie may for this time now and times to come conduct a life unfettered by the dark demands of others, uninfected by poisons of the past. All the early injury, all the damage, it did not go away or disappear. It all happened, it is a fact. There is nothing that can change all that, or wipe it off the chart. But those events no longer color or condition Annie's life. By analytic work, Annie was set free. In her work, Annie had many perilous encounters. But she also found inner friends, and she learned about affection as opposed to merely sex. This really is exceptional. One cannot do much better than this in just two years of analytic work.

And in the process of the work some important matters were decided. We now know that Annie will be strong and well. And that Annie will find love.

Given all that happened early in her life, Annie has been lucky. She took some heavy blows, especially in youth, but she hung on, she did persist. And this persistence made the difference. Annie was courageous and committed. And because she was committed, Annie managed to succeed upon the issues where she was tested, the three great issues of every human life.

The first great issue we each confront is the question of our individual integrity. Do we live right and well according to our nature? Do we embrace the finer values, or do we wallow in the muck? On this issue, Annie started poorly but finished fast.

The next great issue we confront is the question of our sexual integrity. Is sex an instrument of love, or does sex serve just itself? On this issue, Annie had to overcome a crippling early education, but she finally did discover that love is the important part, and that sex is right when it operates in service to that love.

The third great issue of every human life is the question of our spiritual experience. Is life just material and mundane, or is life informed by spirit and religion? On this question with respect to Annie, the jury is still out. Annie has just approached the issue. She has discovered the fine blue jewel of her spiritual existence. But Annie has not yet embraced this part of life.

Even so, Annie has achieved something of real value. She is now alive within the two worlds, the world outside and the world within, the world where spirit thrives. So Annie's time to burnish spirit will surely come. She has learned that spirit does exist, and so now she looks for something more in life, something sacred and divine.

In the search for spirit, we are all at times like Annie. We hope for something more in life, something intangible but valuable. We search for spirit, but we find it not within our ordinary lives. We know not where to look. We know that something is nearby, just out of reach, but we do not know how to get there.

Well now we know! We get there by means of dreams. We discover spirit in our dreams.

But to live with spirit, we must commit. We must make the last and final leap into a life with dreams. If we can make this last long leap, then we greatly do enlarge our lives as we find within ourselves another realm, one which is in every way religious.

This is the great reward of the internal work. We challenge fate and gods to save ourselves, and then we go out beyond ourselves to discover spirit and religion. As a result, our lives fill up with beauty, peace, and purpose as we set our feet at last on holy ground.

This is now where Annie stands,
on holy ground.

Ready now to rise into her duty.
Ready now for destiny.

◊ ◊ ◊ ◊

6

ANOTHER KNOWLEDGE

A MORE
EXCELLENT WAY

The neglected anima

6

ANOTHER KNOWLEDGE

The truth is
what works.

William James

*T*HIS KNOWLEDGE THAT WE HAVE OF DREAMS, this knowledge that served so well for Annie as she changed her life, this is all new knowledge. New in this century. New in our world. But the strange thing is that this new knowledge was at one time understood and then forgot.

Before the time of the Enlightenment, the importance of dreams was common currency among all men and women everywhere. Examples abound. References to dreams are scattered through the Bible. Black Elk, the medicine man of the Sioux, saved his tribe by heeding dreams. In Persia, families traditionally discuss dreams at the beginning of each new day. Shakespeare's work teems with dreams. But the advent of the scientific mind obscured the great significance of dreams. As a result, dreams are undervalued in our overly rational

Western world, and we are poor in matters of the heart and of the spirit. It is to our shame and discontent as modern men and women that we have lost the ancient understanding of things supreme. Now, however, help has been provided. The importance of our dreams has been rediscovered and restored.

Three Doctors

Before the twentieth century, the spiritual life of the peoples of the West was readily contained in the religions of the day. But this container was cracking. Nietzsche and Dostoyevsky told us that God was dead, and Robert Louis Stevenson and Mary Shelley made it clear that the dark side was on the rise. Then, in the first half of the twentieth century, human beings trashed all their common values. Mass destruction was carried out on a scale unprecedented in the life of man. As a result, the fundamental doctrines of ethics and religion were called seriously into question. The world in which we live seems to have no rules. We are left naked and afraid with no principles to guide us. As the devil said to Ivan in *The Brothers Karamazov*, if God does not exist, then everything is permitted. Then in 1947, Sartre observed that it no longer mattered whether God was dead or was alive. We human beings are here in this hard world, and we must find a way to live together without exterminating one another. We ourselves must find a way to discover principles. We ourselves must find a way to spiritual awareness.

To our surprise, we have found that dreams provide the way to both. And this new discovery springs from the work of three doctors, Drs. Sigmund Freud, Carl Jung, and William C. Dement.

Freud

Freud is a towering figure in our century. He is best known as the founder of psychoanalysis. With singular devotion, he worked to understand the internal apparatus of the human being, and then to disseminate his discoveries. As a result, his ideas have infiltrated all aspects of modern life. His great achievement was the understanding that human beings have something inside themselves, a "subconscious" mind. This subconscious is different from the ordinary awareness of the ego complex. And Freud understood right away the crucial fact that, if there is an inner apparatus, then the life inside must interact with the ego complex, and that this interaction has important consequences. Others before Freud had made note of an inner arena. But they did not thoroughly investigate the connection between the life inside and our feelings and behavior. Freud saw that this connection is important and that it produces significant results in actual life. But it was difficult to see this subconscious and its effects. There had to be a mechanism wherein the subconscious mind would show its face.

Dreams were the way. Freud found that dreams were the mechanism of the subconscious. In dreams, he could see the interaction between the life inside and our waking life. In dreams, he could apprehend the peculiar properties of the subconscious.

Freud published his ideas in 1900 in his landmark book, *The Interpretation of Dreams*. This book was a bombshell at the time. It shocked the world with the revolutionary idea of a subconscious mind, a life inside. And it represented the founding of the new science of psychology, the talking cure. This talking cure was a great departure, for, in psychology, the doctor listens to the patient, not the other way around.

Freud had a great impact in our world. His new science of psychology changed the framework for the understanding of the human species. We all recognize today that inner issues affect our lives. We all now are familiar with the idea of a psychic life. However, just a century ago, these things were not a part of knowledge.

Among other things, Freud taught us that inner conflict yields emotional upheaval. He informed us that we can be damaged by trauma incurred in childhood. He saw that slips of the tongue and humor can reveal the inner inclination. Freud also made the more important point that dreams are "the royal road" to the unconscious. However, somewhat surprisingly, Freud did not continue on that road. In later years, Freud disregarded dreams in preference to his other method known as "free association."

Despite Freud's substantial contributions, there are some problems in his work. Freud was most interested in the sexual aspect of human life. He made many fine and interesting theories related to the sexual drive. For Freud, everything in life revolved around the sexual instinct and its impact upon how we feel and what we do. Nevertheless, intervening years have demonstrated that some of Freud's theories are not correct. Freud failed to explore thoroughly the internal world. He saw it only as a basement or a trash heap where one might throw away unwanted items. This is incorrect. The unconscious is in fact a living and creative matrix, the source of life itself, the foundation from which the ego complex and all awareness rises. In addition, Freud was only half right about sex. We have learned at least that there are some important things in life aside from sex. We have learned at least that human beings also have a spiritual dimension.

Another problem in Freud's work is that it is based so rigidly on the medical model. For Freud, there was a right way for humans to work, and, if we did not work that way, then we needed to be fixed. He called the relationship between the analyst and client a "transference," and he used this transference like a lever to manipulate the client's mind, to fix the client so that he or she would henceforth work correctly. This point of view now seems outrageous to some who practice in the field. We find that people are different and unique with a great variety of origin and experience. There is no "right way" that the human system works. It works in many ways. We do not presume to "fix" anyone. Whatever fixing happens comes in dreams from the life inside each individual person.

Because of these flaws in Freud's work, it fell to others more fully to explore the inner apparatus.

Jung

Jung and Freud worked together in the early part of the twentieth century. They first met in 1907. For about six years thereafter, they were close associates.

During that time, Freud, Jung, Alfred Adler, and others of their group were major participants in establishing psychology as a legitimate discipline. But Jung developed some new ideas about the inner system which differed from those of Freud. As a result, Jung and Freud parted company in the latter part of 1913.

Jung's work is even more important and more valuable than that of Freud. It can only be compared in the twentieth century to the work of Albert Einstein. As Einstein explored the external universe, Jung explored the inner world. As Einstein explained how external forces work, Jung explained internal forces.

Jung agreed with Freud that the human creature is subject to an inner system. Jung called this life inside the "unconscious" to signify that it was not something inauthentic or subordinate. And Jung agreed with Freud that dreams were the product of the life inside and the point at which the inner system and awareness intersect. But Jung disagreed with Freud that the life inside was devoted exclusively to sex.

After Jung left Freud's orbit, he undertook to accomplish three essential tasks. He made a thorough survey of the inner system. He learned to decipher dreams. And he made a record of his work so that others could comprehend and replicate what he had done. When he died in 1961, he left us more than 10,000 printed pages as a record of his efforts.

Jung conducted his exploration of the inner system during the period of 1914 through 1918. He descended into the very deepest recesses of his own unconscious. He found that it was not just a bin of trash. Instead, it was dynamic and alive, an arcane realm full of robust forms, natural force, and strange and dark companions. This experience was overwhelming to Jung. It took him a decade to understand what he had discovered. He worked and worked to comprehend what he had found and, with the help of Marie-Louise von Franz, he read old Greek and Latin texts in order to compare his own experience with that of others from the past. Moreover, Jung was first and foremost a clinical doctor. He had patients. He was wise enough to let the patients teach him what it took to make them well. The patients always spoke of dreams. And dreams brought.better health.

Jung slowly did begin to comprehend the outlines of the human personality. In an effort to determine why he and Freud approached their work so differently, he examined types and functions, that is, the introverted type as opposed to the extraverted type, and the functional opposites of feeling and thinking, sensation and intuition. His book, *Psychological Types*, was published in 1922 and created an immediate stir in professional circles and also in the wider world.

Jung did not achieve his overall comprehension of the internal world until 1928. With the assistance of a book of Chinese wisdom called *The Secret of the Golden Flower* sent to him by Richard Wilhelm, Jung finally understood what he had seen within his inner exploration. He then recorded his ideas in a commentary to Wilhelm's book. In his commentary, Jung made the point that the inner apparatus and the ego complex must exist as partners in this life but early on are split apart and therefore come in conflict. He suggested that what we call neurotic symptoms are actually efforts of the inner apparatus to heal the breach between itself and the organ of awareness. He observed that dreams perform this healing function. This understanding was to guide the balance of Jung's life and work.

Jung then undertook to write down what he had learned. Because of World War II, his written work was for a time confined to Europe, then slowly spread to other continents. His *Collected Works* were published in America from 1953 through 1982, one volume at a time, through eighteen volumes, a bibliography, and a general index.

Jung's work is filled with new perceptions. He was the first to describe the "complex." He explained how types and functions affect our relationships with others. And he found that men and women differ greatly as a matter of psychology as well as by anatomy. But Jung's contributions are actually more basic than these new ideas. Jung discovered and described the structure and dynamics of the internal world inside each one of us. He demonstrated how instincts affect us every day, and how archetypal images guide our lives. He taught us that the internal psychic system is an objective and separate reality. He identified our companions that live within the inner system. In a more general sense and with great significance, Jung discovered that we all contain inherited and collective gifts from preceding generations which contain and condition every individual life. We are not men and women with no history or predisposition. We come into this world with temperament and with the knowledge and experience of our ancestors written directly into the central nervous system. We are therefore not just a random event. Each of us is an exponent of our predecessors, and we pass on what we store inside ourselves to the generation which we next create. Thus we are a link from the past into the future.

In the long view, Jung made two discoveries which have proved to be of paramount importance.

First, Jung understood that dreams are messages from the inner system up to the ego complex, and he learned to decipher dreams. As a practical matter, these are discoveries of immense importance for each of us, for they enable us to look at our own dreams to see the problems in our lives. Then we have a chance to reply in ways that make things better, to break the cycle of struggle and destruction and make a better life.

And second, Jung discovered that the inner psychic apparatus is deeply involved in religion, and that our religious interest is just as real and consequential as is our interest in the sexual adventure. He observed that there was a sacred aspect to the life of each of us which we can only find in dreams. This, too, has great practical importance. Toward the end of his life, Jung confided to a friend that, in his clinical experience, none of his patients was ever fully healed without undergoing some form of spiritual renewal.

Dement
Dr. Dement has added the final piece to the puzzle. For many years, he has studied sleep, and he thereby did discover the mechanics of our dreams.

Freud and Jung both worked under serious limitations. In the early part of the twentieth century, no one understood the workings of the dreaming mind. No one knew if we all had dreams. No one knew how dreams occurred. This forced Jung and Freud to bridge wide gaps by theory and by intuition. Many people said, and sincerely did believe, that they did not dream at all. Thus dreams were seen to be of dubious reliability. But Dr. Dement has demonstrated otherwise. He began to study sleep in 1952. As a medical student at the University of Chicago working with Nathanial Kleitman, he studied the rapid movement of the eye which occurs some of the time while we sleep, which we now call "REM sleep." Dr. Dement found that we all experience REM sleep every night, and that during REM sleep we all dream.

Dr. Dement also discovered a universal pattern of sleep which takes place in each of us. This is a cycle of about ninety minutes in which from ten to thirty minutes consists of dreaming sleep. He found that the brain is active all night long, and that, in dreaming sleep, the brain is actually more active than when we are awake. It seems that the brain timeshares itself. By day, it addresses issues in the outside world. By night, it turns to inner business and to internal purpose, and for this it runs internal programs. One of those internal programs provides that we shall dream.

By these discoveries, Dr. Dement established once and for all that we all dream each night, four or five times a night. The only question is whether we remember dreams. Many of us do. All of us can.

In 1963, Dr. Dement moved to Stanford University where he now conducts the Sleep Disorders Clinic. Dr. Dement's work is empirical. He carries out experiments to find out what is really going on with sleeping people. He does not rely on theory, he demonstrates the facts by test and observation.

Dr. Dement has demonstrated many facts not known before. He has shown us that the natural human sense of time is twenty-five hours per day instead of twenty-four. He has discovered that, without external clues and given opportunity, we will sleep ten hours before we will awaken. He has found that we have a sleep bank like a bank account, and that we can be in balance or in deficit. He has discovered that, without an adequate amount of sleep, which is at least an even balance in the sleep account, the human system does not function well, and that accidents occur.

Dr. Dement's work has taught us also that, without our dreams, we all would come unhinged. He has run experiments in which volunteers were allowed to sleep, but not to dream. When REM sleep began, these people were awakened. After some of this, the volunteers began to have unusual symptoms. Although they had substantial time asleep, but no dreaming sleep, these subjects could barely be awakened. And when they finally were awake, hallucinations flowed over them. A similar experiment was performed with rats. The rats just died. From such experiments, we see that dreams are an essential part of every human life.

With his experiments, Dr. Dement completes the work begun by Freud and Jung. Together, these three doctors have shown us that we all dream each night, and that dreams have important purpose.

The discoveries of these three doctors are fundamentally important, and each is to be honored for his work. But these discoveries do not belong to these three doctors, or to any disciples who come after them. They belong to all of us. These discoveries are not "Freudian" or "Jungian" or even those of Dr. Dement. What these men have shown us is just the way the system works. It is the human system. It works the same for all of us. It always has. And it affects all of us every day, whether we approve of it or not. We might all, therefore, be better off to learn to live with it.

A New Perspective

We who work with dreams are more like Drs. Jung and Dement than Dr. Freud. We are clinicians. We have little interest in fine theories. We care about the outcome. Analytic work is practical work. Work of serious consequence. We are engaged with a real person in the real world in real time. We care about what happens to that person. Nothing counts except that the client's life should get better. So in concert with the client and by means of work with dreams, we engage in demolition and reconstruction; we burn and then rebuild.

Like Annie, many people suffer accidents in life which cripple or disfigure. The damage of the accident cannot be made to go away, but it can be left behind. The analytic work gets past the accident and restores each person to his or her original dynamic. For the client, this work is of the utmost consequence. This is how life gets back on track. Therefore, good intentions have no weight. Results count. So the only thing that matters in the clinic is what works.

And in the clinical setting, dreams work. Dreams set the agenda and disclose the problems. And then dreams change our life, not for just short-term return, but for a permanent revision, for a difference that does endure. And sometimes there are other indirect results.

Sometimes the client's health improves. Old illnesses remit. Hope is restored. One becomes expectant.

And then in the clinic we find another unexpected fact, that the life we lead in this external world is not original, but is derivative. In other words, our external life is a reflection of conditions in the world within. This has real and serious repercussions. If we are well and healthy in our inner life, then things outside will be all right. But if our internal world is in upheaval or in disarray, then we find calamity also in our waking world. Thus we have sound and practical reasons to be attentive to our dreams. If we watch our dreams and respond with honesty and courage, life will work out well. But if we ignore our dreams, things go bad and then get worse, and we miss out on the larger more important purpose of our lives.

Therefore, as clinicians, we no longer take in just the sick and damaged for attempts to make repairs. We no longer just do triage and throw the client back into the battle. We still do that in what is known as managed care or in brief therapy. But that is just a band-aid on a broken limb. That kind of work has some value, but is not the best that we can do.

We now treat the injured normal who have creative lives to live, but who have somehow come undone, or have wandered off their better way. We take in those who seek the spirit and cannot find it within their daily lives. We show them where to look inside themselves.

Men and women have always scoured life for spirit. We have tried one thing and then another over long millennia to find this aspect of our own existence. Now we have a way unto the spirit that is open to all of us all the time, a way that works, the way of dreams. Thus analytic work is now accomplished not just to make a pain to go away, but also for the promise of the future, and for encounter with the spirit.

But, despite the gains, not so many undertake to work with dreams. The results of the work are not well-known, and the work itself is difficult and requires time and effort. This is a problem because the human creature seems to be a little lazy. We prefer to walk downhill. When life appears to function well enough, when life flows by with only tiny rips and tears around the edges, we think we do not need to look inside. It usually takes catastrophe to change our minds.

Unfortunately, all true wisdom rides in upon a broken bone.

And so it is that only those who fall into a burning ring of fire are moved to go to work with dreams. But once we start the work, we see that dreams add massive value to our lives. Dreams reflect us now and as we were and as we will become. Our lives become a story. Each day conveys a new and yet surprising chapter. Each night delivers up new dreams of murder or of mayhem, or perhaps of love and hope.

To one who is not intimate with dreams, these results from actual analytic work may seem improbable. Without experience, there is no compelling proof. Accordingly, before we go to work with dreams, we can believe or not believe. There is no objective evidence one way or the other. But when we have lived and died with dreams, when we have been subjected to their power, when we have seen results in our own lives, it is no longer then a matter of belief or of persuasion. It is no longer an intellectual exercise or a scientific question. It is experience. It is a fact. It is an avalanche of facts. And no amount of argument or logic can force the facts to change or go away.

These facts affect your personal decision. When it comes to work with dreams, send not to know what or whom you should believe. Instead, sign on to work with dreams yourself and make your own assessment. Only so will you ever know what value dreams may have for you. Or what value you may have within yourself for your people and your time.

Thus far, only a few have become aware of this new knowledge of the point and purpose of our dreams. These are the modern pioneers, the founders of the future. But they are not exclusive. They seek companions of like mind. They call to you and others:

Come and be a pioneer.
Come and change your life.
Come and break the way for those that follow.

Come to all of this
by means of dreams.

◊   ◊   ◊   ◊

◊

◊   ◊

◊

7

RULES FOR DREAMS

BECAUSE IT HURTS
TO HIT YOUR FINGER

A woman who fought back

7

RULES FOR DREAMS

Imagination
is more important than knowledge.

Einstein

*A*s we have seen with Annie's dreams, dreams can change our lives. And yet, there is the old problem. Dreams don't speak our language. Accordingly, we need to find a way to comprehend what it is they try to say.

In order to understand our dreams, we must realize that the human system is actually quite simple. It is of two parts which need each other. Our awareness needs the life inside for its vision and direction. The inner apparatus needs external life in order to express itself in the world in which we live. These parts crave to be connected. If not, they make war. If so, then they unite in joint enterprise to make of life the best that it can be. It is therefore important that these parts should be attached. And we link these two disparate parts by means of dreams.

In our work with dreams, we find that they are not confined to just this world of time and place. Dreams range widely all around, backward into distant history, forward to the future, outward into an unknown universe. They seek our best results for the life that we will lead. They seek also something more. A life of spirit and religion.

As we move through life, dreams forge the way for us. They are always just ahead. They have a sense of possibilities already predetermined. Dreams thus move us into the future as they disclose to us parts and pieces of coming tides and tidings. If we are quick, we can catch a glimpse of these fragments from tomorrow and so in dreams obtain a preview of what waits for us around the corner.

And dreams challenge us. They drag us face to face with all the central questions. They carry us to storage vaults of ancient understanding. They pose to us the points of right and wrong. They stretch out to the breaking point all our personal capacities. They do not accept our second best. They call us to our finest effort. They demand all we have to offer, and then they ask for more. But they are not so clear in their demands.

As observed in Chapter 3, the messages in dreams are not sent in dry and tepid words. They are wrapped in pictures and in stories. Consequently, we are required to reeducate ourselves. We must learn another language. We must learn of analogue and simile. We must learn to mark the metaphor.

This effort is important, for, if we can read our dreams, we can redirect our lives. Dreams tell us things about ourselves we never knew, things unsuspected, things in stark contrast to old assumptions. But the hard part is to distill the message from the medium. In this we do not do well at all. We have been told too long that dreams have no importance, which is outrageously untrue. Dreams in fact are critical to life. It is essential that we comprehend them or life gets off the track. So for understanding dreams some hints or rules would help. Some guideposts in the night would help.

One who is an analyst learns these hints and rules by trial and error. Over time in analytic work, with many dreams of many men and women of many races, creeds, and cultures, an analyst is called upon to comprehend. And, after while, the rules for reading dreams become apparent.

But most of us have no such hints or rules. We are untrained and therefore unprepared to deal with dreams. We do not know the language. We do not know the grammar of the game. But there are pointers and some clues that can help us decode dreams. There is a discipline and rules that help to translate the images of dreams into words that we can understand. However, there is no place that I know of where these rules are written down. So to help the interested reader, I here write down the rules that I have over years distilled from dreams.

The rules which follow are not exhaustive nor are they definitive. Others understand dreams differently and may also be correct. There may be rules that are forgot or not yet formulated. And the rules expand as we and others learn and write down more. But the list below will be a start, and it is pretty good. Besides, we need not understand each and every dream. If we can just get half of them, we will be exceptional, and half will be enough.

The rules written down below are not imposed by outside force, or by authority. They do not come from books or institutions. These are rules deduced from actual effort, and they come to us at heavy cost in terms of tears and dark despair of the many who have gone before. These rules spring not from theory or from doctrine. They spring from life, from actual facts. These rules are true only as experience, and because they correctly do reflect the nature of the creature.

These rules are natural laws, like gravity, or that it hurts to hit your finger with a hammer. They are rules because they work.

We need to learn these rules. If we are to be free, we must understand and then apply these rules. In order to achieve a truly independent life, we must someday decode dreams alone and so become our own lifelong analytic partner. This is the whole point of the analytic work, that we should be self-sufficient in this life. These rules may help us to that task.

The Rules for Dreams

ONE: *The life inside reflects to us the face that we have shown to it.* If we express by how we live hatred or contempt for the life inside, then it responds in kind. On the other hand, if we show respect and due regard for the world within, then it will welcome us. This life inside is like Diogenes. It walks at night searching for the strong and reverent man or woman. It will sometime in this life examine us. If we prove to be one of special promise and commitment, it will favor us in life and lay upon our doorstep gifts and second sight. If, however, we are corrupt or coarse, the inner apparatus will abhor us. There are not many rules in this life that are absolute, but this rule is one, as are Rules Two and Twelve.

Two: We cannot with impunity defy our own nature. When we first burst into this world, we are fixed and formed by our genetic gifts. We have a natural design, a path, internal values, anatomy and temperament. But this can be obscured. As we grow up in life, due to environmental factors and to external stress, we may deviate from the natural line inside. We may begin to live in ways that are foreign to us. We may break away from what is truly ours to live a life decreed by others. We can do this if we wish, but only at a cost, for in such a case we soon become a toxin to ourselves. Our own true nature will then despise us. We become an allergy to our own existence. We have a sort of psychic lupus. Then life goes awry. We get hurt. We get sick. But the inner system does not easily abandon us. It will tug upon our sleeve to pull us back to our right way. If we respond, then life will flow again. But if we fail to heed the quiet voice inside, if we are such a hard case that even getting badly bent makes no dent upon our minds, then disasters continue to occur. The risk is then extreme. Accidents can kill, and bad things in the body sometimes cannot be cured. And such bad things occur because we live in ways that defy our own design, in ways that insult our natural gifts.

THREE: Dreams are education. Each of us comes to maturity with no knowledge of the life inside. And yet, this inner life is the consequential aspect of our whole existence. In order to live correctly according to our own original blueprint, we must be connected to this life inside. Dreams do this. Dreams connect us up and then explain us to ourselves. They show us what it means to be outgoing instead of introspective. They bring us intuition or reality, whichever in waking life we lack. Dreams measure data by intellect or feeling, whichever otherwise is absent. In dreams, we wrestle with instinctive life, with animals inside, and then with archetypal force. In such titanic struggles, the outcome is unknown. Sometimes we win, sometimes we lose. The important point is that we are engaged, and that we learn from each of these encounters. By means of our encounters, dreams deliver to us an unusual education of enormous value. Without our dreams, we are forever ignorant of the most important facts of our own specific lives. But with our dreams, we know all the time everything we need to know.

FOUR: Dreams are introduction. The complete personality of each of us consists of several component parts. But we do not know them and they are not acquainted with each other. Therefore these different parts run around without coordination. They tend to trip over one another, and they often are at odds with us. But these inner figures are not always evil or pernicious. They also are inspiring. In dreams we meet these other aspects of ourselves. We have direct discourse with them. When we meet such a figure in a dream, he or she may tell us vital facts which we need to know. So when you meet companions of the world inside yourself, when you have a chance for frank exchange, be sure to ask the four important questions: *Who are you? Where do you come from? Where are you going to? What do you want from me?* The answers to these questions can guide your life for years to come. So listen carefully and follow what these inner figures say. If we ignore the counsel of the inner figures, we must prepare to be abused. But if we follow their advice, the inner figures will help us realize all the better aspects of ourselves, and lead us also to the spiritual adventure.

FIVE: Dreams are real. As stated earlier herein, dreams are just as real as are events in our external world. In other words: *The internal world is real.* It is objective. It is consequential. It is only difficult to comprehend because it is reflected in our dreams in metaphor. What we can do in dreams, we can do in life. If we can weather a storm in a dream, we can weather a storm in life. If we can cross a great chasm in dreams, we can make a great change in life. Thus the life we live inside is fantastic but authentic. What we do there prepares the way for everything we do within our waking world. And dreams tell us precisely where we stand within our waking world. For example, a young woman dreamed that, as she graduated with her high school class, a nuclear missile blew up the campus and obliterated everything except herself and her best friend. The actual facts were almost as dramatic. Her life was changed as certainly as if by nuclear explosion. In another case, a man dreamed that his ship ran aground and broke apart. However, the splinters of the wreckage turned into little motor boats so that all aboard returned safely to the shore. There was in this dream some bad news and some good news. For the bad news, the dream said pretty clearly that the life this man had lived was lost and gone. It had run aground and broken up. But the good news was that no important parts were lost. All the passengers on board were saved. This is the actual position in which this man finds himself. His life has come apart, but he can rebuild. He can make a new and better life, and this time, perhaps with help from dreams, he will not run his ship upon the reef.

SIX: Dreams are dialectic. We have a dialogue with dreams. They come by night. We respond by day. We respond by how we live and in our attitudes. We reply by decisions that we make, and by our conduct. The inner system recognizes our response, and then replies by means of other dreams. We thus see dreams change and move around as time goes by. They comment on our life and we react. As we progress, they progress. This point and counterpoint continues for a lifetime. New topics are considered. New events are calibrated. We find that life is a series of experiments. Some work, some fail. In dreams we see the difference. We can then terminate experiments gone bad; we can then pursue experiments which have worked out well.

SEVEN: Dreams form the roadway for our lives. There is seldom a specific right or wrong for the experiments in life. There is instead a range of possibilities, choices as to time and place and then degree. But there are limits, points of no return, borders which we need to see. Without dreams, we go past the borders, we go too far and then get hurt. Dreams show us these points of no return. Dreams reflect our individual boundaries. In dreams we see the margins of our natural path. We find a channel. We wander down the road between the walls. If we go too far one way or the other, we hit the wall and bounce back into the middle. Thus dreams keep us to the centerline of our proper course.

EIGHT: Dreams have to do with us. Our dreams rise in the context of our lives, and most of them have to do with us. Thus in dreams we learn much about ourselves. We see in dreams conflict or cooperation. We see approval or rejection. For example, in a dream a young man arrived at home to find another man in his bed. He was so outraged that he attacked the man, gouged out his eyes, and threw him off a cliff. What a bad reaction! This young man had to undergo a serious readjustment in order to accept within himself the presence of the inner figures. To his credit, he did just that, and thereby greatly did enlarge his life. Dreams also give us information from the outside world which we need to know. As a man considered a transaction with a stranger, in a dream he saw the stranger smile, revealing the two rows of teeth of the great white shark. Because of this dream, the dreamer passed on that affair, which later proved to be a huge disaster. In another dream, a woman saw that in my office four of us were waiting for her there, two men and me and one related woman. At first she was put off by the loss of privacy, but then she understood the dream was telling her that she had my full attention, and all of my best efforts. This is how we learn. We look at dreams, and then we draw conclusions. This is important because, in ordinary life, we have no way to be objective about our own inherent value. We suffer from a judgment that is partial, a judgment that is colored by the bias or demands of many other people. To fit with them, we do what is popular, or what seems to be expedient. But the life inside has a better, broader point of view. It knows what is right for us. It knows our best direction, what kind of person we are meant to be. Therefore we need our dreams in order to discover our own reality. The commandment is to "know thyself," and the only way to know oneself is to know your dreams.

NINE: We never know another unless we know his dreams. Unless we know a person's dreams, we know only bare appearance. The real stuff is out of sight and all inside.

So be careful when you pick your friends, for we can never know another person if we never see below the surface, if we never see his dreams. But we must also be aware that dreams are private and important property. If someone makes a gift of dreams to you, they must be handled with the greatest care. The dreams of others must never be discouraged or disparaged, or sent back in heated argument as a dart, or as the poisoned point upon a hostile spear. We must be reverent with our children's dreams, or with the dreams of husbands, wives, or lovers. Such dreams should be greeted with respect and serious consideration. And then, because of dreams, we may have a truly intimate acquaintance with someone for whom we care.

TEN: Dreams tie us to people that we love. As we sleep, the facts of other lives flow across to us in dreams on bridges of emotion. Important knowledge comes to us at night concerning parents, husbands, wives, our children, and others who are linked to us by means of our affection. As one example, a man was awakened by a dream that his son was sick and far away. He said to himself, "What has happened to my boy?" A few hours later, he received a telephone call long distance from his son who was indeed in a dangerous condition. Such dreams are fairly common. We all dream of those we love, and we see them in our dreams as they really are. This is useful, and yet it has a curious result. Infidelity and other crimes cannot be kept a secret. When people sleep together, internal information seeps out at night and crosses over. One absorbs the guilty knowledge of the other. Therefore, if we wish to pursue something like an extramarital affair, it may be better just to tell our spouse the truth. Honesty is always a requirement for a healthy life, and anyway, he or she will know what we are doing soon enough. In dreams, the one will see the other in the very act of his or her betrayal. Even if the dreamer does not remember dreams, the image will clank around within the mind like Hamlet's father's ghost, and with similar results.

ELEVEN: *In dreams, we sometimes see the future.* It seems that dreams are tied into a web of time and fate laid out just in front of us. Therefore in dreams we can catch a glimpse of what is yet to come. And so sometimes at night we see around the corners. Examples of this phenomenon abound. A man who was married to a flight attendant dreamed that her airplane crashed. In a panic, he got out of bed and called the airport, but there was no report of any difficulty with her flight.

However, within the hour, her airplane collided with another. Both planes crashed and everyone aboard was killed. A boy dreamed of his best friend waving as he went away. The boy's best friend was ill and died that night, but he had come a final time to say good-bye. A man whose son was in military service in a foreign land dreamed that his son came home for one last farewell. This made no sense to the dreamer. But in a surprise attack that night, this man's son was killed.

TWELVE: Nothing is sacred to an unsatisfied life. This is a powerful rule, and all too accurate. If we ignore the call of the life inside, it will smash everything we value. Absolutely nothing is sacred or off limits. That which we cherish most will be most certainly destroyed. This is why it is so important to respond to dreams. If we work within our dreams, we may disarm hostilities before external bloodbath. But if we ignore dreams of conflict or demand, the altercation moves outside and becomes destructive in extreme. For example, a man was most unhappy in his marriage, and dreamed about it many times, but chose to take no action. Within two years, the marriage came apart in a spectacle of wreckage and of ruin. Things eventually turned out all right for him, but this man might have spared himself much pain and agony had he responded earlier to dreams. He learned the hard way, better to cope with ugly truth within our dreams than meet disaster on the street. If we work things out inside ourselves, we may be called upon to sacrifice, but we at least maintain some semblance of control, and we avoid complete abject defeat.

THIRTEEN: Dreams are simple and direct. Although they speak in metaphor and simile, dreams say exactly what they have to say. They are not diffident or timid. On the contrary, they are honest to the point of being brutal. They are spontaneous and independent. Their whole intent is to bring to us important information which we need to know. They speak to us as plainly as they can in the only language that they know. In pictures and in stories, they inform us of what is hurting us. This is quite a gift. As earlier observed, if we do not know the problem, then we have no defense. But dreams show us a picture of what it is that makes the pain, and then we have a chance. We can respond. But do not expect too much from just a single dream, or from just a few. Dreams are more like pieces of a puzzle. One piece does not a picture make. But when the many pieces are in place, we can see the pattern. So do not approach your dreams as if they are complicated or enigmatic. They are just stories with a point. Take them in symbolic form, but take them at face value. And do not be too optimistic or sanguine. Assume the worst. Dreams do not sugarcoat our lives. They tell the awful truth, and they are sometimes really grim. But they are not nightmares to be forgotten or dismissed. Every dream is of value because it transmits knowledge. And knowledge is a power that we can use to make our little lives take wing.

FOURTEEN: Dreams work. For an understanding of ourselves, and for substantial change that does endure, dreams yield good results. They have real advantages. They rise inside of us, not from a foreign source. They come every night. They repeat. They correct themselves. They come with continuity. They will not hurt us. They seek only our best interests. If we fail to understand them, they come again and then again until we get the message right. Other forms of work may cure a symptom, but that is not enough. The symptom merely moves around. If one can manage to stop smoking but does not cure the underlying problem, one may then take up drink or drugs. Symptoms shift and change, but causes remain the same. Dreams ignore the symptoms and focus on the source. In this the dreams are unrelenting. They cannot be bought or fooled. They go directly to the root. They continue to attack until a result has been achieved. And this result will last, for when such work is rightly done, it rightly will endure. No other form of work is so readily available, so accurate, or of such consequence. No other form of work will last us for a lifetime.

FIFTEEN: Dreams are not so hard to understand. This is the great secret. Dreams are not that hard to understand. Dreams are stories. They have players, plot, and resolution. Therefore, in order to understand a dream, we need only recognize the players and then compare the beginning of the dream to the ending. Consider this example. If in a dream someone is chasing us, and he catches us and cuts us up, then we have a conflict and we are losing. This is not a good result. But if in the dream we overpower our opponent, we are much better off. We may have a conflict, but we will overcome. With respect to adversaries in our dreams, we should remember this. Hostile figures who appear in dreams will not kill us in the dreams (although they may kill us later). They know that, if we are dead, then also they are dead. So we are always free to fight in dreams, and we must always fight against the dangers in our dreams. At worst, we wake up in a sweat. At best, we overcome an adversary and move into the future. In either case, we must wake up and write down our dreams in detail. Don't think about them now. Think about them later. The most important thing is to get them down while they are fresh. When we later pick them up and consider them at length, we will find that we can reduce the meaning of each dream to just a single sentence. This is how we process dreams. We extract and then refine the message of the dream until it is just a single simple sentence.

SIXTEEN: Dreams are destiny. Dreams move us to the future. They precede us. They break the way. They pull us through the brambles to put us where we need to be. They summon up our best potential. They seek the whole and most we have to give while we are here. Thus dreams call us to our destiny. If we will rise to meet that destiny, we live long and well and with effect and with reward. We live then a life that is quietly extraordinary, a life that is the gift of dreams.

By means of work with dreams, we sow ourselves into this world, we spend ourselves with purpose and with design. Our life becomes a tuning fork. As we ring out, other lives ring too. If we ring well and truly, adjacent lives ring in tune. But if we ring a sour note, nearby lives also ring off-key.

So you see, one life does make a difference. And dreams carry you to that specific difference which you can make by your own life while you are here. But be forewarned. Of those to whom special gifts are granted, special obligations are exacted. When we step into this new dimension that results from work with dreams, we find our lives are no longer ours alone. Our lives now have consequence for others.

We live then not only of and for ourselves,
but also of and for our family and our friends,
of and for our people and our time.

And of and for the life inside,
the life of spirit and religion.

◊   ◊   ◊   ◊

8

ANNIE'S STORY — POSTSCRIPT

TO BEGIN
AGAIN

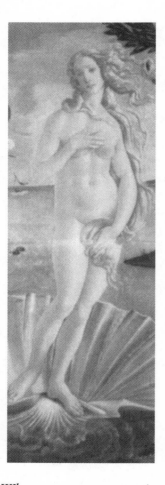

When a man pays attention

8

ANNIE'S STORY — POSTSCRIPT

No coward soul is mine,
No trembler in the world's storm-troubled sphere . . .

Emily Brontë

So, WE ASK, how is Annie doing now? After years gone by, how has the work held up?

Annie is just fine, thank you very much. Alive and well and looking forward to the new adventures of her life as she continues on the inner exploration and applies the knowledge of the life inside. She exhibits all the signs of analytic work well done. She feels good. She is healthy. She has nice dreams. She is happy, more or less. Her life is working well, and it has kept the promise made to her in dreams. Love has come to Annie, love and marriage, and family of her own. And equally important, Annie has found direction for her future, long-term purpose for the life that she will live.

Annie was most fortunate. Her life might easily have gone the other way. She was seriously at risk. But she was young and strong. More important, she was honest and devoted. These qualities of character carried her. Character, as we say, is destiny. Therefore, despite occasional lapses and mistakes, Annie persevered to great success and now has much to which she can look forward. All because of work with dreams.

Dreams showed Annie that she had been abducted in her youth by hostile forces which came from the family hearth. These destructive elements expressed themselves in Annie's life as too much sex and too few feelings. Everything was material, nothing was religious. Annie was called upon to separate from family and reorganize her values, but she could not easily accept that task. So in dreams Annie crashed, and the crash did real damage. It led in Annie's dreams directly to despair, despair to suicide, and when an inner sister saved her from herself, a crazy woman came in a dream and tried to murder her.

Annie somehow survived all this, and also gathered strength. In her dreams, she withstood earthquake and invasion, emerging stronger than before (thus proving what Nietzsche said). Annie was proving herself. She earned admiration and respect from the life inside and so received a most magnificent gift, the best gift she could hope for, a second chance at life.

But more trouble was on the way.

A longing for the family put her in a dream up a tree and on the swing out of control. Refusal to make a choice put her through the dream of the lightning storm. Both were very dangerous events. Had she been not quite so dedicated, Annie might here have given up. But Annie held on. Another dream then brought to her the fine blue stone of her spiritual life, and in a later dream she discovered her own treasure island of individual development.

A recent dream reflects Annie's present posture. In this new dream, Annie found a picture of herself from some years back. In the picture, Annie's teeth were in bad shape. They were rotted out, completely covered over with rank and rancid slime, and her mouth was full of sores and awful dread disease. Then in the dream Annie looked into a mirror. She saw that now, at this present time of life, her teeth were strong and fine and clean and white and straight and bright. She was looking good. This was an important message to Annie from the life inside. It said she once was ill, but is now completely cured, all out of work with dreams.

From dreams and the analytic work, the guard of Annie's prison ship became the man in search of new religion. The occupants of Annie's tenement became her helpful sisters. And the small stone wall too puny to protect her became the building that will never fall. This is how dreams reconstruct a damaged life.

For Annie and for now, life is good. But the vicissitudes of our mortality have not all just gone away. There are always ups and downs in life, triumph and disaster, forks upon the road. There is always pleasure and pain, folly, and excessive obligation. But whatever rough beast comes now around the bend, Annie meets it straight ahead and unafraid. She is not undone by suffering, nor is she fooled by rapture. She no longer lives within a prison of illusion. In all events, she maintains an even keel.

So now we may fairly ask: What can we learn from Annie and her dreams? Well, we can learn a lot.

First, when we are not connected to the life inside, we are flying blind. We have problems with ourselves and we are dangerous to others. But when by means of dreams we connect up to the life inside, we heal ourselves and we no longer injure friends.

Second, when we explore the world we have inside ourselves, we meet companions with whom we share a common bond. And they have a special understanding. They have seen first hand our own discrete design. They know our natural capacity. They see the better way. They urge us on to all our better efforts. They help us find the road that is just right for us. Then our lives light up, and things in general work out well.

Third, the world within provides a passage to the world beyond. We there discover powers that we never knew, powers we did not imagine. We sail out then to meet and to confront those larger powers.

Finally, we are by those powers tried by fire and tested. If we pass through our examination, if we are found to be both worthy and devout, we are then enlisted in the everlasting struggle to express in this hard world in which we live the practical vitality of spirit and religion.

For making use of what we here have learned from Annie, life is very democratic. Each of us has dreams each and every night. But the question always is: Who will respond? Who will do the dance with dreams? Who will wrestle with the life inside?

And then the question turns distinctively to you.

Will you respond?
Will you engage the life inside?

Will you answer to
the call of dreams?

◊   ◊   ◊   ◊

◊

◊   ◊

◊

9

THE GRAND DESIGN

THE NATURE
OF THE BEAST

The sacred marriage

9

THE GRAND DESIGN

You are not wrong to deem
that my days have been a dream . . .

Edgar Allan Poe

*T*HE PSYCHOLOGY OF THE HUMAN CREATURE is quite simple and straight forward. Some who write in the field make it seem complex and difficult. But it is not. It can be summarized in the following eight ideas.

FIRST: The adult human personality is not a unitary system. It is divided into two important parts. One part is the organ of awareness which we call the ego complex. This organ governs our conscious life over which we have some dominion and control. The other part is the larger psychic apparatus out of which awareness does arise, which for each of us is the source of life itself. This larger apparatus is unknown to us, so we call it the unconscious. We find it internal to ourselves, and we go there in our dreams. We therefore refer to it as the inner system or the life inside.

SECOND: When we are born, as a matter of psychology, we are only instinct and archetypal knowledge. Our awareness develops slowly over time. It is constructed bit by bit in youth and adolescence. It is limited and conditioned by genes and by our temperament. It can be either injured or improved to some extent by our environment. When fully formed, our awareness is quick and agile, elastic and expansive, adaptable and versatile. However, as compared to the life inside, it is small and frail, has restricted vision, and is all too easily deceived and damaged. But even with such imperfections, this detached awareness is the great achievement of the human species. Without this cool awareness, we would only be a primate.

THIRD: The inner system is quite different from awareness. It is the reservoir of who and what we are and can become. It contains our original design, our natural inclination, and elements of fate. It is genetic and endemic. It is the molten core. It is slow and hot, immense and indestructible. It contains intrinsic disposition, the aggregate of talent and capacity, all the possibilities of life. It is connected and provides a gateway to planes outside ourselves, to universal values, to all anterior experience, to whatever is divine.

FOURTH: In early childhood, everything exists in an undivided but instinctive concert, as in a soup or in a stew. This is a happy state, an unperceiving unity. But as we grow up, the birth of our awareness destroys that accord. This great mutation splits the early wholeness into the two component parts, the ego complex and the life inside. This division is at once the source of inspiration, and also the cause of deep distress.

FIFTH: For any life to work out well, awareness and the life inside must play their proper roles. These roles are quite distinct. The goal of the life inside is to express itself in the world of our reality. It is the source of all important enterprise. It is then the role of our awareness to carry forth and implement the initiatives of the life inside. This is why the ego complex is so important to the process. Small and frail it may be, but it is the only passage through which the life inside may move into the world outside ourselves. Accordingly, the ego complex must understand its function, must see the new initiative, provide it form and structure, and pour it forth into the world in which we waking live.

SIXTH: Problems arise at the birth of the ego complex. Things become confused. Parents, siblings, churches, schools, the social order, wars and revolutions, accident and misadventure, desire, lust, ambition, greed; all these impinge upon the growing child and may arrest or misdirect, cripple or distort the young awareness. We may no longer know what belongs to us and what belongs to others. Due to ignorance or to irreverence, or to excessive scientific education, we no longer realize that we are the subject of superior wisdom. Our awareness then naturally esteems itself too much, grows prideful and oppressive, and goes off on frolics of its own far from original intent. We have disconnected from the life inside. Life in the outside world then becomes a hazard. We lose our way. We fall into bad company. The internal apparatus tries to call us back, but we no longer hear, and may no longer care. Life becomes in this event problematic. The inner system then may seek to do us harm or do us in, disaster sometimes follows hard upon disaster. Worst of all, we lose our capacity for inspiration.

SEVENTH: The only cure for this affliction is that the organ of awareness must turn around and reengage the life inside. This frequently requires the ego complex to let go of a misdirected life, to sacrifice what it has so that it may grow into a better form in accordance with its original design. To the limited perspective of the ego complex, this will seem a painful task and the loss will seem unbearable. However, this sacrifice is the necessary step to a larger more rewarding life, for it enables awareness and the life inside to reconnect in harmony and in common purpose. This reconnection, though, is not a simple job. It cannot be done directly. It can only be accomplished indirectly by means of work with dreams.

EIGHTH: This reconnection of the organ of awareness to the life inside is the important purpose of our dreams. Dreams have been designed by nature to connect awareness to the inner system so that, in adult life, the two maintain a parity. Dreams flow up each night from the world within and to the organ of perception thus to fuse together these two disparate parts. Dreams tie the two together as coextensive counterparts at work in joint enterprise so that we can do the best we can with what we have while we are here. Thus dreams provide an elegant solution to the basic problem of the split inside. Nature created our awareness so that we could rise above the brute, but this had a very bad effect. It split awareness from the life inside. So nature made a cure. Nature made dreams to heal the split. Dreams bridge the gap between the two important parts and so enable us again to function as a whole. Dreams connect us up once more to universal values and to the realm of spirit and religion.

The foregoing eight points are a summing up of how our system of psychology seems to work. If you can grasp those eight ideas, you will have the tools to know yourself, and to rise into your larger life. And you will see that the most important questions in any human life are always these:

Do you remember dreams? By means of dreams, does awareness live in harmony with the life inside? Do the two work as partners in joint enterprise? Or do they live at daggers drawn?

If awareness and the inner system live as strangers or as enemies, then life will go all wrong. One is in that case a victim, one's life becomes perverted. As a result, one does damage to himself and to others whom he loves. But if awareness and the life inside abide as friends, as companions hard at work in joint purpose, then one takes up the great adventure. One embarks upon an expedition into all one's better efforts. One will engage this world, and yet another world beyond, the world of the spiritual experience.

This is why dreams are so important. By means of dreams, we reconnect the two parts of our personality. Thereby we heal ourselves. We then construct a larger life wherein we rise above common cares and commonplace concerns. We go to meet the living spirit, and the living spirit enters and illuminates our full existence. All of life is then inspired by a sense of mission and of meaning, and by a profound inner understanding. We are then no longer merely human. We have entered then into a new estate. We have become somehow a piece and particle of whatever is divine.

So you see, when you work with dreams, you have it in your hands to make something really special of yourself. Dreams create the fully integrated personality with all the pieces in the proper place, all working in the proper way, in unity and harmony, in service to the whole, and to the universal force. The result is most remarkable, something fine and rare, and it yields a most extraordinary life.

A life mundane and yet majestic.

A life both existential and religious.

◊   ◊   ◊   ◊

◊

◊　　◊

◊

10

DREAMS

LIGHTNING
IN THE NIGHT SKY

Encounter with the spirit

IO

DREAMS

Saintly people saintly seem,
but do not saintly dream.

A voice within a dream

*I*N ANNIE'S STORY, we have seen how dreams affect the single dreamer, how dreams can change our lives. This is, of course, the most important part of analytic work, that is, how dreams affect the dreamer.

But it also is instructive to see a large array of dreams, the dreams of many men and women over a large expanse of time. Then we see how dreams usher in the future, how dreams express the universal values, and how in dreams we may encounter spirit.

Famous Dreams
Some dreams are quite well-known. The most famous dream in America is probably Lincoln's dream of his own death. In early April of 1865, Lincoln dreamed that people were weeping in the White House. He went into the East Room where he saw a catafalque bearing a

corpse in funeral vestments. He asked, "Who is dead in the White House?" A soldier replied, "The President. He was killed by an assassin." Within days thereafter, Lincoln was shot and killed by John Wilkes Booth at Ford's Theater in Washington.

Fifty years later, a similar event occurred in Europe. On the morning of June 28, 1914, Bishop Joseph Lanyi, who had been tutor to Archduke Franz Ferdinand, dreamed of the Archduke's death. In the dream, the Bishop found on his desk a black bordered envelope addressed to him from the Archduke. In it was a picture and a letter. The picture showed young men firing pistols at the Archduke and his wife as they rode in an automobile through a crowded street. The letter read as follows: "Dear Dr. Lanyi, I herewith inform you that today my wife and I will fall victims to an assassination. We commend ourselves to your pious prayers." It was signed by the Archduke in Sarajevo at 3:45 A.M. The Bishop awoke at just that time, wrote it all down, called in others, and said a mass for his ill-fated friend. As we all now know, this dream came true, and World War I began.

Christopher Columbus also had a dream about his future, but with a better outcome. While in Portugal before setting sail on his historic voyage, a voice in a dream whispered to Columbus this reassuring message: "God will . . . give thee the keys of the gates of the ocean." Columbus set sail westward from the Canary Islands on September 6, 1492, in search for a passage to the Indies. In the moonlight of October 12th, a deck-hand on the *Pinta* sighted the island that we now call San Salvador in the West Indies just off the southern coast of America.

Creative Dreams
Dreams are the source of much creative inspiration. Many writers have drawn from dreams. Yeats based his 1902 play, *Cathleen ni Houlihan*, on a dream. This was an explosive work regarding Irish independence which set in motion events that culminated in the Easter uprising of 1916. Mary Shelley's *Frankenstein* came to her in a nightmare. Robert Louis Stevenson first saw the dark side, Mr. Hyde, in a dream, whom he then described in his book, *The Strange Case of Dr. Jekyll and Mr. Hyde*. John Masefield copied his poem, *The Woman Speaks*, directly from an engraving which appeared to him in a dream. Dreams also traffic in music. Handel heard the last movement of *The Messiah* in a dream. Richard Wagner found his opera, *Tristan und Isolde*, in a dream.

Political strategies can come from dreams. For example, Gandhi's idea for nonviolent mass strikes, which eventually led to India's independence from British rule, came to him in a dream in 1919.

Science and commerce also sometimes become the subject of dreams. In 1865, while searching to discover how carbon atoms were arrayed within a molecule of benzene, Friedrich A. von Kekule dreamed of several long rows of atoms which looked like snakes. Suddenly one of the snakes seized hold of its own tail and began to twist and turn in a circular motion. Von Kekule awoke with a start, and also with the critical understanding that carbon atoms are arranged in a closed ring, a discovery that revolutionized organic chemistry.

Elias Howe for many years tried to make a sewing machine with an eye in the shank of the needle. He met with constant failure. One night he dreamed that savages took him prisoner and demanded that he invent a machine that could sew or else he would be put to death. He failed again, and the savages raised their spears to kill him. Howe noticed that each spear had an eye at the tip of the point. He awoke and understood that this was the answer to his problem. When Howe placed the eye at the tip of the needle, the modern sewing machine became a reality.

Dreams of Organized Religion

Dreams have always been important in religions. It is recorded in *Genesis* that Joseph correctly interpreted Pharaoh's dream of seven fat years and seven lean years and so saved Egypt from famine. Generations later, in a dream reported in *First Kings*, God agreed to give Solomon whatever he asked. Solomon asked only for an understanding heart so that he would be a good leader for his people. God was impressed. He granted Solomon's request, and then, because Solomon had asked for nothing for himself, God granted him also riches, honor, and long life.

In the second verse of *Matthew* in the New Testament, Joseph, the husband of Mary, was warned in a dream that Herod had sent soldiers to find and kill the baby Jesus. He was instructed to flee with his family into Egypt. Joseph heeded those instructions and took his family into Egypt where they lived for many years. Then in another dream Joseph was told that Herod was dead and that he should now return with his family to Israel so that Jesus might fulfill his prophecy. Once again, Joseph was faithful to his calling. He returned into Israel with his family, Jesus came of age and lived and died in the Holy Land, and the Christian religion was born.

In the Buddhist religion, which arose six hundred years before the Christian era, in a legend much like the Immaculate Conception, Buddha was conceived in a dream when a white elephant descended from heaven and pierced the side of his mother, Queen Maya, with one of six tusks. Thus the Buddha, like Jesus, was born of divine impregnation unstained by original sin. In Islam, Mohammed was instructed in his divine mission by means of a dream. He recorded the dream in great detail in the fourteen chapters of his book, *Nocturnal Journey*. This dream and this book provided the spark from which the Muslim religion was established.

Dreams of Ordinary People
The dreams described above are striking, but they are no more powerful or telling than the dreams of the everyday person. Here are examples of two dreams from ordinary people not in analytic work.

A man in Woodside, California, dreamed that he would win the lottery that day. In answer to the dream, first thing in the morning, he went to a store and bought five lottery tickets. Two won a total of seven dollars. With those seven dollars, he bought seven more lottery tickets. One of these paid the jackpot for the day, five thousand dollars. Score one for dreams!

The following dream describes quite precisely and without any pity the exact position of a woman with respect to her internal world. The dreamer was the same woman who dreamed about the ring of fire, an attractive and articulate woman in the middle part of life. About a year before she began her analytic work, although apparently happy and successful, she had a warning dream. In the dream, she was at sea on the deck of a submarine when it suddenly submerged. She barely made it back inside. The submarine was under attack. It was immediately blown up by depth charges. All hands were lost, except the dreamer somehow managed to escape. She bobbed to the surface, adrift at sea with no raft and no resources. She saw an island in the distance and began to swim. After an exhausting effort, she finally made it to the island and crawled ashore. But a man was waiting for there and attacked her, absolutely in a frenzy to kill her. She fought back, and killed him instead. Even so she was still not safe. As the dream ended, soldiers were after her, under orders to find her and to kill her.

Two things are obvious from this dream. First, in her inner life, this woman is under serious assault. She and the inner system are not at all on friendly terms. In her life outside, this woman must be living in some way that contradicts her natural sense of order. Second, this woman has courage and better possibilities. At every dangerous event, she fights back. She is resourceful. She survives.

This woman eventually undertook to work with dreams. In the time since she began, with rare honesty and courage, she has weathered huge storms in life and made substantial changes in the way in which she lives. As a result, she no longer has dreams of death and harsh destruction.

Dreams in Analytic Work
Sometimes life starts out on the wrong foot. The early structures are crooked or deformed. Then in analytic work those early structures must be dismantled and rebuilt. This, too, can be seen in dreams. A man about fifty, whom we shall call Mr. Able, dreamed at the beginning of the analytic process that he got aboard a gigantic bulldozer with a blade the width of several city blocks. He cranked up this giant bulldozer and then knocked down all the buildings in the neighborhood. He cleared the whole area, razed it to the ground. This done, he could begin the work to reconstruct.

In the course of his analytic work, Mr. Able had other important dreams. In the first of these, he found himself walking along a rocky trail in the wilderness. He stopped at a stream for water. A voice startled him. He looked up to find a strange bearded man, a hermit, speaking to him. The hermit identified himself as the Keeper of the Trail. He asked Mr. Able if he were traveling to the Three Mountains. The dreamer replied that he was not sure where he was going. The hermit laughed at this honest answer. He told the dreamer that most people wander around for a while, but soon enough make their way to the Three Mountains to take up residence on one of them.

When Mr. Able and I discussed this dream, I made the suggestion that the Three Mountains might be greed, ambition, and lust. These are the three great powers that capture most of us. I suggested that there was a Fourth Mountain, a place of enlightenment, a place of spiritual awakening, and that Mr. Able could forego the Three Mountains in search of the fourth. Mr. Able liked this idea, and he did indeed set out in search of the Fourth Mountain.

Three weeks later, Mr. Able had another dream about the mountains. He found himself back on the rocky trail and he met again the hermit. The dreamer told the hermit that he was not going to the Three Mountains because he had a friend who had told him about the Fourth Mountain. The hermit laughed again and told Mr. Able that he had a smart friend. The hermit also told the dreamer that he would have no trouble finding the Fourth Mountain, just follow the trail. He added, however, that one cannot get to the Fourth Mountain directly, that he must go over or around or through the Three Mountains. It would be a lot of work. The dreamer sighed and said that he had been afraid of that.

Following a brief rest, Mr. Able set out on the next leg of the journey. After a long walk, he could see the Three Mountains looming in the distance, but the Fourth Mountain was still not in sight. Presently, Mr. Able came to a large gate across the trail. A huge man, the Gate Master, guarded the gate. The dreamer asked the Gate Master if he had to do anything special in order to pass through the gate. The Gate Master said no, all you had to do was ask. Mr. Able asked and the gate swung open. As Mr. Able passed through the gate, the Gate Master asked him if he were on the way to the Three Mountains like everybody else. The dreamer said no, he was looking for the Fourth Mountain. The Gate Master smiled and told the traveler that he was very lucky, that most people do not know about the Fourth Mountain and so settle for one of the others. However, the Gate Master also told Mr. Able that the Fourth Mountain was hard to achieve, and that he had ahead of him a long and difficult journey. As a last act of kindness, the Gate Master gave the dreamer a cup of water. Mr. Able drank, gave thanks, and began again the long journey to the Fourth Mountain.

Are not these splendid dreams? Is not this man headed in the right direction?

Another man of similar age, one Mr. Baker, had tried before to find a way into his inner life. But not anything he tried would work. Then he discovered dreams. In one of his first dreams, Mr. Baker found himself at the edge of a deep chasm, a place where he had been before. Previously, there were only two ways down. He could either jump, in which case he would be killed, or he could climb down on ropes through poisonous gas, in which case he would be killed. A Hobson's choice. But now in this new dream, Mr. Baker saw that there was now a third way down. There were steps cut into the face of the cliff through a safe area. If he were very careful, he could descend step by step, dream by dream, all the way to the bottom of his own internal world.

Mr. Charles, near the midpoint of his life, made a similar discovery. He dreamed that he came late to a train station. The train was already pulling out, and it was the last one. In desperation, Mr. Charles managed to leap on to the last car as it was leaving the station. Out of breath and gasping for air, he found himself aboard and in the presence of an unexpected fellow traveler, a beautiful woman who was very interested in him. Mr. Charles was fortunate. He had just barely managed to catch the last train out, his last chance to become acquainted with his own internal world, and with his feminine companion. Had he missed this last train, he would have missed an important part of life.

Dreams of Trouble on the Way

Sometimes the analytic process does not run quite so smooth and slick. A woman in her late twenties, whom we shall call Ms. Delta, was doing fine work, but then went away on a long vacation. This vacation seemed to break her concentration. Shortly after Ms. Delta came back, she had the following dreams in rapid succession. In the first, she was playing hockey, but her goalie kept knocking the puck into their own net. In the second, she was on an elevator which got stuck between floors. In the third, she was on a raft hooked to a helicopter which was pulling her across a lake. The raft broke loose and sank, and she nearly drowned. In the last, she was on a boat going backwards down a river. The boat ran into rocks and broke apart, dumping her again into the water. Obviously, at the time of these dreams, Ms. Delta was headed in the wrong direction. She herself understood the dreams completely, and by means of extra effort quickly turned herself around. She now continues with skill and resolution the search for her better possibilities. In more recent dreams, in reward of her good work, Ms. Delta has been given a raise in pay by her superiors, and she has received letters of praise and of appreciation. At this point for Ms. Delta, things are good and getting better, and she has every reason to look forward to her future.

Families sometimes block individual development. I was working with a man of about forty who was very admirable, one Mr. Easter, but whose life had somehow been stymied. One night, after visiting his family, he dreamed that he was driving along a highway in his car, but the road was blocked by a gigantic red lobster with huge and grasping claws. Here it was. Life had been blocked by a clinging parent. Over time in his actual life and also in work with dreams, Mr. Easter worked hard to make his way around this formidable creature. Eventually, he got all the way around and in the clear. In practical effect, he got some distance from his family. Thereafter, he was able to enter into the full catastrophe of life, with all its risks and hardships, and all its wonders and rewards. Love occurred, and then a marriage, then a child and then a home, and all the while a job. Because of work with dreams, Mr. Easter managed to achieve all that which in early life he had been denied.

Another younger man, one Mr. Fox, found himself in a similar fix. He dreamed that he went home for a visit and found waiting for him in the backyard of his parents' home a giant vampire bat. The bat was very hungry, and had every intention of feeding on Mr. Fox. But Mr. Fox was a smart young man. He was out of there. Sometimes you just have to stay away from the family zoo. This is what Mr. Fox had to do and what he did. And thus he spared himself many a battle with that gigantic vampire bat.

A young woman, one Ms. Granger, was in a similar position. She dreamed that her mother and her father were sitting in the living room reading the newspaper. It was a quiet, nice, domestic scene. However, her brothers and her sisters lay in the four corners of the room, mutilated, dead, and dying. As you can see, this was not a healthy home. And like most of us, Ms. Granger did not escape unscathed.

Sometimes family attachments can have very bad effects. I once worked with a woman in her twenties, Ms. Havasu. She was quite close to her father, who was divorced. But then her father remarried. Ms. Havasu dreamed that, at her father's wedding, she discovered blood dripping from her fingertips. She examined both of her hands and discovered to her horror that there were shards of glass under all her fingernails, all ten of them, all the way up to her elbows. She began to pull them out. As you might imagine, the pain was terrible. From this dream, we can see just how traumatic it was for Ms. Havasu to see her father remarry. But she was bright and strong, and she recovered. She continued on her own path and created for herself a life that is full of challenge and adventure.

Sometimes it is just too late to correct a family problem. I worked for a period with a young man I liked very much. We will call him Mr. Iomac. Mr. Iomac had grown up in harsh conditions in which he had been subjected to a lot of trauma for a long time. In the analytic work, Mr. Iomac dreamed that he was walking at night through a dark forest when he fell into a pit. The pit was full of black water and black and poisonous snakes. He tried desperately to climb out, but the pit was too deep and the walls too steep. As he thrashed about, the black snakes swarmed over him and bit him repeatedly, hundreds of times. The dream ended here, with Mr. Iomac still in the pit, still covered by the snakes. This was a very bad ending which made me fear for him. Three days later, Mr. Iomac suffered a psychotic break. He was hospitalized and then placed on a program of drug therapy which will, of necessity, last for him a lifetime.

Dreams of Inner Figures

Dreams are most intense when one approaches inner figures. The first we usually find is the shadow, the dark side of who and what we really are. A pious man might in a dream look in a mirror and see the devil, or some other incarnation of utter evil. An industrious man will dream of bums and hoboes. Nice women dream of prostitutes. Prostitutes dream of librarians or of school teachers. Such dreams are not to be taken lightly. The dark side has real power and can be quite deadly. We might reflect on Annie's dream in which the dark side tried to kill her.

As well as the dark side, we meet in dreams the contrasexual soul.

One Mr. Jackson took up the analytic exploration and did fine work, which required that he contend with dangerous powers. In one early dream, as he was coming out of the ocean, Mr. Jackson was attacked by a giant alligator. In pitched battle, he managed finally to prevail. Like all experience in dreams, this battle was real within the confines of Mr. Jackson's mind, and the outcome here was very positive. This fierce combat prepared Mr. Jackson for the next step in his journey.

In a later dream, Mr. Jackson climbed down into a deep cavern to find and rescue his feminine soul, who had been there imprisoned for all the years of his adult life. Mr. Jackson searched and searched and finally found her, but the way back up was impassable. Mr. Jackson and his feminine companion therefore had to travel further down, down into the dark unknown, down into the pits. Deeper and deeper down they went, not knowing where they were or what they might encounter. But Mr. Jackson pressed on, his courage and determination never flagging, guarding and protecting the woman at every step along the way. Just when it seemed that they were lost, they caught a glimpse of light. They followed the light to its source and there found an exit from the cavern by the side of the sea, hard by the surging sea. This was a great success for Mr. Jackson. By his courage and resolve, he found and then set free his contrasexual soul.

Mr. Jackson's dream is the dark hard journey every man must someday make. A man must find and then release his beloved feminine soul. By what he did in this dream, Mr. Jackson saved himself from becoming too rigid and too hard. He discovered and rescued his contrasexual soul who embodies all the natural wisdom and the feeling values at the core of his existence. He thereby greatly did enrich his future life.

As this dream illustrates, a man must discover and submit unto his feminine companion. She will then imbue his life with all the vast array of understanding and compassion which she carries in her heart.

Women must also meet their inner masculine companion, but the way of this is vastly different. Whereas a man must save and then submit to his internal soul, a woman must at first fight the animus. If she asserts herself, the woman will prevail. Then the internal masculine companion becomes her ally which has wonderful curative effects within the woman's life and brings great potential for her future. The following dreams show what must be done.

A woman of about thirty, Ms. Kelso, early in her analytic work, dreamed that she was pursued down a dark street at night by several savage men. She was brave. She fought back. She had a gun and shot them many times. But this did not even slow them down. They just kept coming. Finally, she ran to a nearby house, and the woman who lived there took her in. As the dream concluded. Ms. Kelso had managed to find a place of temporary safety. But this battle is not over. Ms. Kelso will meet these men again. This dream illustrates the great task of a woman's adult life. She must fight the inner masculine forces that would dominate her. If she will not fight this battle inside herself, then she will meet destructive men in the world outside, and she will have recurring problems in relationships for which, of course, she will blame others.

Another woman, whom we shall call Ms. Loran, met the same problem with more success. In a dream, she was living on the frontier before the turn of the century. Hostile Indians attacked the settlement. She was badly battered by one of the attackers. She was saved only by the aid of others. This attack left her very much afraid. She knew that hostilities would come again. But, because of her analytic work, she knew also that she could do something to save herself. In another dream, Ms. Loran tracked down the young warrior who had so badly battered her. She went in peace to speak to him. She explained that he should not attack her, that he should help her in her life. It turned out that this young warrior was pretty nice. He was not so sure how this would all turn out, but he at least agreed to try. As a result, relations between the ego complex and the inner system were much improved, and Ms. Loran's life reflected this advance.

A third woman, whom we will call Ms. Mason and who was a little older (which tends to be of help), had even better luck. In a dream, she went to visit a man who kept a large red snake in a swimming pool. Once in a while, the snake would get out of the pool and walk around as an alligator. The alligator/snake could be a danger to Ms. Mason, but the man was in control and was very careful to protect her. He explained all about the creature to Ms. Mason and made sure that she was safe. This is just what a woman needs from her masculine companion: care, concern, and safety; and connection to the mysteries of the life inside.

Recurring Dreams and Vivid Dreams
Recurring dreams, or vivid dreams that awaken us, are signals of important messages. In a recurring dream, the inner system sends the message up to us again and then again until we understand and then respond. In a vivid dream that awakens us, the message is so important that we need to get it right away and then right

away take action. The following dreams are but two of many examples of recurring and intense dreams.

A man had several dreams over the course of a year that he was shopping for a new car. In his outer life, although his automobile was not brand new, he was satisfied with it. He had no intention to replace it. But then he was in a minor accident, and later his car encountered some unexpected mechanical problems. And so, indeed, he found it necessary to purchase a new automobile. And then this dream did not come back. When we understand the message of recurring dreams and then respond thereto, they go away. So it was for this man. Once he made the purchase of a newer car, the dreams of shopping for a car disappeared and never did not come back.

The dreams that scare you wide awake are quite important. The woman who dreamed of the ring of fire and the sinking submarine had another dream of consequence. In the dream, she fell out of a car on a busy freeway and was run over and dismembered by a truck. In the dream, she saw her body parts rip off and fly away. As you might imagine, she woke up in terror. But this dream turned out to be a gift. As a result of it, she began her analytic work, the results of which have changed her life.

Dreams of Sacrifice

In work with dreams, one is frequently called upon to give up things. For example, Ms. Mason was instructed in an very early dream as follows: "Old things must be destroyed before new things can take their place." This was a call for sacrifice, and for restraint from her propensity to self-indulgence. It fell quite hard on Ms. Mason, for she was forced by dreams to abstain in life from things she dearly did desire, but which were bad for her. But she was a woman of substance, and she did what was necessary. As a result, her life bloomed in other aspects that she never could imagine.

This requirement for sacrifice is very hard for most of us to bear. We are loathe to let go of what we have and what we prize. And yet, in analytic work, the loss of what we have is a prerequisite to the advent of what will come. This point was clearly put to Ms. Kelso, the woman who in an earlier dream had a shooting match with internal men. She and her daughter were living with a man, but not agreeably. It was a tense, unhappy situation. In a dream, Ms. Kelso was in bed with the man. There were dead and dying birds in a nearby cage and a fire broke out below the bed. To the deep distress of Ms. Kelso, this dream said that this relationship was dead and also about to burn. She took the hint.

She soon left the man, and her life thereafter expanded in ways that were quite surprising to her.

A dream also helped Ms. Kelso help her daughter. In the dream, Ms. Kelso caught her masculine companion peering up her daughter's skirt. This was quite shocking, and it was having very bad effects in her daughter's life. Ms. Kelso had to fight this masculine figure in order to protect her daughter. With bravery and with a mother's love, Ms. Kelso fought him to a standstill. Thus she saved her daughter's future. Now, years later, both Ms. Kelso and her daughter, and her daughter's children, are well and active and engaged in all the challenges of life.

Dreams that Have Effects

Work with dreams has powerful effects. Sometimes physical effects, sometimes emotional effects.

A woman in her thirties, Ms. Randall, came to analytic work in an effort to combat a long, intractable eating disorder. In the first month of analytic work, the illness went away, and it never did come back. I have also seen this happen with other forms of illness.

Ms. Randall was a strong and intelligent woman who in short order cleaned up her life and made of it something really fine. However, from time to time she had some trouble with the masculine element. In one dream, she and other women were on a roller coaster at an amusement park. Roller coasters in dreams are not good. They are much like Annie's swing, they represent an unstable situation. The man who ran the roller coaster was a problem. He kept turning it on and off, jerking the women around and keeping them up in the air. A classic case of a disruptive animus. Finally, the women had enough. They got out of the roller coaster seats and climbed across the metal framework to the man who was the operator. They attacked him with a knife and killed him on the spot.

This attack upon the man who ran the roller coaster was very good. When elements in dreams do damage to us, we need to kill them if we can. Better elements then will come along to take their place, and life will lighten up. Indeed, as a result of what she did in this dream, Ms. Randall's life directly did improve.

After this dream, Ms. Randall did well for quite a while. Then she met an actual man who got attached to the dark side of her internal masculine companion. This is a risky proposition. As a consequence, things got weird again. Ms. Randall dreamed that she had made a mess, which she surely had. She dreamed that young boys from the wrong side of the tracks did some great athletic tricks. This was, of course, the sexual acrobatics. And then something really bad happened. While carrying a small child in a dream, Ms. Randall fell into a whirlpool in a stream and got sucked down to the very bottom. She and the child managed barely to survive, but it was clear that she was in for danger and destruction, which did actually occur. Although Ms. Randall's relationship with the man in her external world had certain of its own rewards, in the end it was also very painful and very costly.

Long-term work with dreams has one effect which may be somewhat surprising. The marriage rate for women who work with dreams has been high. Except for women who were previously long-married, or who in dreams are drafted to an separate destiny, many of the single women who have engaged in long-term work with me have met with love and marriage. And many, like Annie, have had children. This is an interesting development. These women, because of work with dreams, may have become more compatible companions. And there is one more important point. These women will be better parents. They will avoid mistakes that other mothers make for lack of knowledge of the life inside. They will not suffocate their children. The children of these mothers will have a chance to grow

up straight and strong and unmolested by the renegades and dark desires of a mother who is not aware.
And these mothers can also teach their children early
on the joys of their dreaming world.

Dreams and Error

Sometimes we set out on a course of conduct that is
bad for us. However, once embarked, we seldom look
back. Dreams, however, call attention to our errors.

For example, a woman was involved with a man
who was toxic to her. However, she was addicted to
him and would not give him up. One night, while
sleeping with this man, the woman dreamed that she
was her daughter and had married a criminal. Right
away we can see three things from this dream. First, the
woman is behaving immaturely. She is, like a daughter,
naive and reckless. Second, this woman is committed.
Marriage is a big step. And third, the man is not
sound. He is rough and dangerous. In the dream, the
newlyweds came home and went upstairs to consum-
mate their marriage. When they did not come back,
the dreamer went to look for them. What she found
turned her stomach. The two had taken razor blades
and cut each other up. There was nothing left except
blood and bone and bits of flesh upon the bed.

Can a message be more plainly put? I doubt it. This dream said to the dreamer in the most dramatic and intense way: "This man is not good for you. If you persist in this relationship, it will yield you nothing but trials and tears and a badly broken heart." This woman is full of good stuff. She got the message. She saw the error of her ways. With the help of this dream, she finally overcame her own addiction.

Things that Dreams Despise

There are two things that dreams do not like, that they consistently do despise.

Promiscuous sex is one. Drug use is the other.

As example of the sexual problem, Mr. Fox (who previously in dreams escaped from the giant vampire bat) sometimes took his pleasure from unknown girls whom he met in bars. He had many dreams criticizing this behavior, but he liked the sex and would not quit. Finally, he dreamed that his inner feminine companion delivered to him an ultimatum: "I'm giving you one last chance, and then you're gone." When something like this occurs, it is of serious concern. This is an internal figure of great power. She can kill, or she can break one's legs. Mr. Fox took notice. He finally gave up his sexual recreation. Soon after, he met a very nice woman with whom he fell in love. He is now married and has made for himself a fine career. He has also with his beloved made a family of their own. So you see, as this example illustrates, there are reasons and rewards for living right, and there are penalties and punishments for depravity.

Dreams hate the use of drugs even more so than promiscuity. For example, the use of drugs shows up in dreams as electricity burning up one's brain. One on drugs has dreams in which he fights the hydra, or other mythic monsters. One on drugs in dreams is torn asunder time after time. Such dreams are filled with battle, blood, and gore, and little work that is constructive can be accomplished until the client quits from using drugs. One simply cannot do analytic work when one is stoned.

Among the many ill effects of drugs is that they bore holes into the brain. They spawn rapacious worms that eat tunnels through the memory system. Another ill effect of drugs is that one who uses does not mature. Drug use stunts internal growth. If at seventeen one begins the use of drugs, and continues unabated for ten years, although he is then twenty-seven, his psychology is still just seventeen. Then life is more difficult than ever. One is retarded. One is always just a little off.

One cannot quite behave as one should. It is a simple and yet dreadful problem. The person that one was at seventeen is not sufficient for life a decade later.

Restorative Dreams

When we are laid low by life, when we have been ill or injured, dreams can repair and restore the damage done. This was illustrated in a dream of Ms. Mason. In the dream, she was both a surgeon and the patient. As surgeon, she operated on the patient and took out all her insides and her organs. She carefully cleaned all the insides and the organs, then filled them up entirely with gold. The surgeon then carefully put everything back inside and closed up the incision. This is a picture of the analytic effort. One is both the doctor and the patient. In Ms. Mason's case, although she had been soiled and injured in the lists of life, she was now cleaned up and restored with all her highest values.

A man in his fifties, Mr. Victor, had real gifts, but also a certain difficulty to see beyond habitual routine. He was informed in a dream that, "The purpose of life is life." From this, Mr. Victor learned that the meaning of life is our actual conduct of life. In a masculine life, we are what we do. Mr. Victor had survived a difficult youth which had misdirected his development. Only later and by means of dreams was he able to define himself and realize his own individual promise and potential. He was then told in a dream that his life had been saved because he was so intelligent, and because he had important work yet to do. In the course of his analytic exploration, Mr. Victor found within himself interests and alternatives which he had never yet considered. With the courage of his convictions and in cooperation with the life inside, Mr. Victor has now thoroughly remade his life in the external world.

Dreams of Spirit

Dreams are at their very best when they lead us to the spiritual experience. Such dreams are always striking and some are quite profound. The dreams that follow are a just a few of those that I have seen.

About two years after Mr. Charles caught the last train out with his beautiful feminine companion, in another dream, he and she and another man were in an industrial city. As they walked through the city, they came upon a smokestack made of old and blackened brick. As they looked on, the black bricks at the top began to break away. Suddenly, in a cascade of soot-black bricks, the smokestack fell apart. To the great surprise of Mr. Charles and his companions, beneath the bricks was a magnificent gold and crystal building, a cathedral, which reflected in its myriad facets the golden light of the midday sun.

This dream was quite an event for Mr. Charles. The cathedral is the quintessential symbol of religion. Mr. Charles had spent his entire adult life in industrial pursuits, very serious and ambitious. Now, abruptly, that whole industrial structure had collapsed and in the bargain revealed that, inside himself, Mr. Charles was really a religious man, something which he had long ignored or never knew. This discovery, of course, had substantial repercussions in the way that Mr. Charles has since then lived his life.

Ms. Mason also made a spiritual discovery in her dreams. She was adrift at sea in a dream when a castle rose before her from the water. It was a fabulous structure that came straight up out of the deep. Elaborate and ornate, it consisted of several tiers plated in pink and gold. Angels were clinging to it, wings beating furiously, as they lifted the castle out of the ocean. As the castle came out of the water, a turret opened at the top. A large and luminous male stepped out. To Ms. Mason, it was clear that he was a religious figure, a living spirit. He was not forbidding or overwhelming. On the contrary, he was quite friendly. He smiled and invited Ms. Mason to step inside the castle, which she did. He showed her through the castle and then they sat down for a long and deep discussion of intricate and abstruse religious issues.

Mr. Fox also found religion in a dream. A few years after he avoided the hungry vampire bat at his family home, in a dream he was swimming in the vast reaches of the ocean, ranging far and wide like a creature of the sea. He noticed that, just below the surface of the sea, there was a white coral-like structure. It was very unusual, and it extended everywhere. But more than that, *it was alive*. It radiated energy and vitality. It had a presence which inspired awe and reverence. And then, quite suddenly, in a flash of revelation, Mr. Fox understood. This underwater structure was the living tissue of whatever we call god, and Mr. Fox was in some way connected to it.

This was a wonderful event for Mr. Fox. He discovered in this dream the divine life that underlies all of our existence. And he discovered that he was a part of divine life, that he was connected to it in some way that he did not fully comprehend, but connected all the same.

Mr. Able also encountered a friendly spirit in his dreams. While looking for the Fourth Mountain, Mr.

Able discovered three colossal buildings which he then explored. In the last one, he found the statues of seven gods. As he examined these statues, the seventh god suddenly became alive. Mr. Able was taken quite aback as this seventh god boldly spoke to him.

The seventh god told Mr. Able that his name was "Phlange," and he named the other gods as well. He told Mr. Able that he was the god of self-destruction and so had been selected as Mr. Able's guide because Mr. Able had been so self-destructive in the past. But Phlange quickly reassured Mr. Able that now, in his search for the Fourth Mountain, he was not destructive any more. Phlange then gave Mr. Able strict instructions. He said that Mr. Able was now engaged in a search for truth. He told Mr. Able that he must be both diligent and persistent in this search, and that, no matter what, he must never quit.

Mr. Able was true unto his task. He kept at it. About six months later, as Mr. Able explored another building in a dream, he met Phlange again. Phlange called out to him, "Hi. Do you remember me? I'm Phlange." Mr. Able replied, "Yes, of course, Phlange, I remember you. What are you doing here?"

Phlange told Mr. Able that he had come to see how Mr. Able was getting along in his search for truth. Mr.

Able told Phlange that he was all right, but that he gets off the track sometimes. Phlange laughed and told Mr. Able not to be concerned, it is normal to wander off from time to time. Phlange then said to Mr. Able, "Don't forget to keep your goal in sight. It is never easy, and it won't get any easier. You just have to keep chugging along." Then Phlange departed and Mr. Able continued on his way.

About three months after this second dream, Mr. Able found himself in a strange and ancient city which he did not recognize. He asked a passerby where he was. He was told that he was in the city of Cassia, in Sumeria. Mr. Able went to the center of the city where he found a fountain. He stopped to drink. A woman noticed him and asked if he were a traveler. Mr. Able replied that he was a traveler, but he was not sure why he was here. The woman said to Mr. Able: "Many people come here. We are known as the City of Truth. Truth seekers come here to study, for we have many fine scribes and truth-tellers." Mr. Able was definitely getting someplace in his search for truth!

Mr. Able met Phlange one last time. In one of Mr. Able's dreams, Phlange appeared out of a white mist and spoke at length. It was an imposing conversation. Phlange told Mr. Able that each of them is just one part of a greater whole, and that the most important point for the greater whole is the force of life that moves. Anything that no longer moves is not alive. Phlange instructed Mr. Able to keep on moving, to embrace each new adventure, thus to be alive. Phlange explained that, when Mr. Able learns new things, the gods also learn. He said that the gods and Mr. Able are all connected, that one is but another aspect of the other. Thus what Mr. Able can accomplish in this life informs also the life that is divine.

Phlange then made an extraordinary revelation. He said that Mr. Able and Phlange and the other gods are all connected to all the people everywhere, and that what we do in this life comes back to each of us again as bread cast upon the water. He called on Mr. Able to do right in life, to treat others well, for what Mr. Able does for others he does also for himself, and for the spirit that lives within us all. Phlange said that, as part of the greater whole, Mr. Able participates in everything that happens in his time, and everything he does affects the whole. Therefore, Phlange called on Mr. Able to spend himself well and truly in this life, for what he does affects the very spirit of the world in which he lives. Mr. Able is now trying with his best efforts to live up to this injunction.

Sometimes a dream comes along that is simply stunning. Ms. Kelso had such a dream. It came on her birthday some years back, as important dreams often do, a beautiful birthday gift. This dream was so striking and so moving that I include it here substantially as Ms. Kelso wrote it down.

I'm in the house of my ancestors. It's old, large and multistoried, an intricate and complicated design. Many people live here, an extended family or a tribe. Outside, there is an electrical storm with lots of lightning. I'm alone in a part of the house where I have never been before. I feel uneasy, fearful. Should I be here? Am I in danger? I'm aware of the storm outside. The air crackles with electricity. It feels surreal, as though the storm is a supernatural phenomenon. I open a door which takes me into an area of several stairways going up and down. This seems to be the major thoroughfare for getting to all parts of the house. I look up a stairway zig-zagging into the unknown regions above me. I see a woman coming down the stairs. I feel a jolt of fear. At first I think it is a ghost, because she seems to be translucent, obviously not flesh and blood. She's large for a woman, but not unnaturally so. She is so fascinating that I cannot take my eyes off of her. The woman wears a dress which seems to be at once both of the past and of the future. It's as though what used to be is being transformed into something yet to come. The dress is serious attire, but not severe. It is long and flowing with some delicate feminine touches. The fabric is dark, not black or brown or blue, but somehow all and none of these colors. The woman seems almost in some way to be wearing a religious habit. It's the clothing of a matriarch, a monarch, or a nun. I want to run away, but I can't. Instead, I am entranced by the woman coming down the stairs. She doesn't walk in typical fashion, nor does she float. She is "walking" down the steps, but in a smooth and flowing movement, all of a piece. Now I can't run away. I would be missing something extraordinary. I simply wait for her. She's ancient but not ugly. The closer she gets, the more stunning she is. She isn't smiling, but her expression is by no means somber. There's a joy behind it and a serenity which I envy. She also seems to be loving without love weakening her. I feel drawn to her and in awe of her. I am won over completely. It is because of her. She exudes unsentimental caring. Her love is real, powerful, and fierce. I know she would never hurt me. It now seems ludicrous that I was ever in fear of her. I step forward to embrace her. As she nears me, she is already telling me many things, instructing me in the ways of the house. I can't say that she is using words, but she's speaking to me in my mind. She reaches my side and puts her arm around me. Her touch is something for which I have waited my whole life. I begin to walk in step with her. I feel like a child on a long-promised adventure. I can't wait to see where she will take me. I am safe with her, safer than I have ever been before. More than that, I feel blessed by her presence. This is unmistakably her house. She has lived in it forever. She knows it, knows everything and everyone in it. I feel her knowledge, power, and serenity. More than sharing them with me, she will help me make them into a part of myself. I am her daughter come to claim the birthright that she has held for me so long.

Such a beautiful dream! It resonates with all the power and the purity of spirit. It is the incarnation of the holy ghost. It is a dream that will inspire she who dreamed it for a lifetime.

Thus in dreams we mere mortals
encounter spirit and religion.

We are so fortunate.
We are made to dream!

◊   ◊   ◊   ◊

II

PICTURES

The Stations
On The Journey

The triumph of the feminine

II

PICTURES

The Good is the Beautiful.
Grant me to be good in the inner man.

Plato

*T*HE PICTURES IN THIS BOOK have been chosen because they so well express the progress of the analytic effort. They reflect step-by-step the stations of the inward expedition, not in words, but in the archetypal image as formulated by the individual artist.

The artist performs a special function for the world in which he lives. He is a pipeline for the life inside. Two qualities distinguish him or her. First, he is good at his craft, whether it be painting or writing, or carving stone. Second, the artist is often peculiarly close to the unconscious. It is as if the ego complex of the artist is not quite strong enough to close the door upon the molten core. Or perhaps the membrane between the two is just too thin and porous. Because of this, inner images rush up and take possession of the artist, and he or she is seized to render them in concrete form.

This circumstance is both a blessing and a curse. It provides the artist with an endless source of inspiration. And because this inspiration comes directly from the life inside, the artistic work will resonate with all of us. However, this unfiltered connection between the ego complex and the life inside may wreak havoc with the artist in his own life, may simply use him up and spit him out, van Gogh and Poe being but two examples.

Those of us who are not so afflicted are the beneficiaries of this phenomenon. We are not great artists, but we can appreciate great art while we may also have a decent life. And we gain an education. With many artists over time, we accumulate a record of the full measure of human travail, and with much more clarity than can be seen in the messy, fragmentary life of the single individual. Accordingly, we now have artistic renderings that reflect the effort for awareness at least as well as words, and perhaps more powerfully.

The struggle with the dragon — frontispiece

The struggle with the dragon is the starting point for all of us. We are in a battle with a monster, a most uneven match. Our little light of individual awareness is up against the huge devouring dark unconscious. This is the same story as Jonah and the whale; the same idea expressed in Goya's painting of *Colossus*. The ordinary man or woman becomes aware of the life inside only when it steps on us. And then it is too late to get prepared. The life inside just crushes everything and then walks on, heedless and uncaring of the wreckage that it leaves behind. We are hard at work in life, and then a dragon ambles in and shatters all that we have built. We are shocked and shattered. But we must always keep in mind: Destruction is the first act of creation.

The paradise of ignorance — page 4

Our ignorance is the problem. We are unaware and undeveloped, living in a prison of our innocence. The dragon comes to bring us education, to set us free. We have lived too long in Eden. So the serpent whispers in our ear that the apple is delicious, and we eat thereof. Unfortunately, this apple conveys the knowledge of good and evil, knowledge which is reserved to God alone. The serpent is for his complicity condemned. But the Gnostics thought of this particular serpent as a higher form of god, calling men and women to become aware, to enter fully into life. However, God of the Garden was very angry. He instructed angels to drive men and women out of Eden lest they eat next of the Tree of Life and so become gods themselves.

The price of our awareness — page 14

As a result of gaining knowledge of good and evil, men and women were expelled from the Eden of their innocence. And so we find in our own lives that efforts to become aware exact an awful price. We are confronted every day by questions of right and wrong, some of which seem insoluble. We find ourselves pulled apart, dismembered, left wretched and pathetic in a harsh and unforgiving land. We may then recall the irony of God's curse to Adam. He said to Adam, "You wanted knowledge, and now you have the knowledge; and that, my son, will be your curse." Thus we poor mortal men and women have been condemned to struggle throughout our short existence with all the awful issues of good and evil. A substantial curse indeed.

The evil of the female — page 48
The dark side of the male — page 68

In order to become aware, we look within. Then we have a shock. We come face to face with our own dark side. In our internal world, we discover a companion who is dishonest and depraved. A woman finds someone like *Medusa*. A man will find the cruel and brutal comrade who is responsible for massacre and carnage, grand and petty theft, and other crimes on the small and epic scale. Before we can go on to better things, we must come to terms with this, the darker side of life. We must contend therewith and come away in friendship, or at least in truce, or we can never go beyond this barrier to the finer aspects of our lives.

The oppressive animus — *page 88*
The neglected anima — *page 122*
As the analytic process moves into the unknown country, we find inside ourselves the contrasexual soul. We see these figures first in uncivilized form because they are unschooled. A woman finds inside a man or men intent to carry her away. A man will find inside a woman impoverished by neglect. This meeting is a point of peril and also opportunity, for the outcome of the analytic effort depends upon success at this important time and place. The woman must resist the inner man and establish her equality. The man must find humility, and by attention and affection raise the inner woman out of beggary.

A woman who fought back — *page 144*
When a man pays attention — *page 166*
When a woman battles back against a hostile animus, she can win. She can dispatch him as an adversary just

as in the picture Judith did. Then other and more positive masculine companions will surface to replace him. These new companions will light her way as she moves forward and help her to achieve fulfillment as an individual woman. When a man pays attention to his internal feminine companion, she will be recast and reawakened as a goddess like Venus or Athena. And she will bring into his life an inner wisdom and composure that he has never had before.

The sacred marriage — page 174
When the inner reconciliation is accomplished, the ego complex and the contrasexual soul may enter into holy matrimony, into the sacred marriage. This is an event of surpassing consequence. By this union in the inner world, all the aspects of the personality are fused into one true and seamless living system, all the parts tied together properly, all at work in harmony and for a common purpose. Life then moves into the future with dedication and resolve, with promise and potential.

Encounter with the spirit — page 184
After the internal marriage, one may advance to the final level of the analytic effort. One may reach the central core of life inside, and find thereat the gateway

to the world beyond. One moves through that gateway into the realm of real religion. One may there discover and embrace the living and dynamic force that is the spirit, and may become an instrument thereof. One then returns into the ordinary world in which we daily live, but now different and distinct as one who carries inside himself a new awareness. In days that follow, wherever one may go, whatever one may do, one's life will be informed by the spirit now that lives within.

The triumph of the feminine — page 224
The heroic masculine — page 234
When a woman or a man is transfigured by union with the spirit, then life itself is changed. It is more substantial than it was, more consequential, full of so much meaning, so charged with greater purpose. Life then becomes a calling, the expression of a more imposing vision. We all can, if we wish, participate in such a life. If we work with dreams, we may become that rare and special man or woman who is reconfigured into someone quite unusual, someone not quite of this world. We are then no longer mere material existence subject to the roar of frenzied instinct. Our lives now teem with obscure knowledge and archaic erudition. Our lives now transcend the personal to the universal.

The divine child — page 238

As we complete the inner exploration, we come full circle. We are reflected as a child again, but this time a child divine. A child to signify that we again will grow into the future; divine because now we carry spirit. And we again do battle with the dragon, but on a different scale. We are no longer overmatched. The dark unconscious is now a smaller reptile, and we are at least its equal. But one thing has been greatly changed! The divine child has brought the duty of divinity, the duty that we fight against the darker gods every day. A duty that we do in dreams, and in dreams prevail.

Landscape with stars — cover

Asleep at night, we see cascades of stars. These stars are the diamonds of our nights, our dreams. Each night, dreams plunge and tumble through our lives, full of feeling, full of meaning, full of all the best we have to give into this world while we are here. Dreams prepare the way for us, and we follow where they lead.

Are not dreams wonderful?

They transport us to the stars.

◊   ◊   ◊   ◊

12

DIAMONDS

THE PITH AND QUICK
OF EVERYTHING

The heroic masculine

12

DIAMONDS

The net of Heaven is cast wide.
Though the mesh is not fine, yet nothing slips through.

Lao Tzu

So DEAR FRIEND, we come to the end of the book. It is therefore time to ask the crucial question: What did this book bring to you?

This question is, of course, impossible for me to answer. For each of you it will be something different, something which has as much to do with you as with the written words upon the printed page. But the book's intended message can be directly stated. You, too, have dreams. You, too, can work with dreams. You, too, can change your life.

When we work with dreams, we live with a foot in each of two worlds, the material world outside, and the world within, the world of sanctified life. We live two lives, the life of the body and the life also of the spirit. And we work in two realms. We work within the daylight world in which we waking run to earn our food and keep, and then we work at night in dreams inside ourselves in our search of universal truth and original religion.

Original religion!

Not conventional religion. Not canon, creed, or dogma. Not church or state or social order. But real religion, religion that courses through our lives each and every day, a power that can never be ignored. Religion that we do not speak. Religion that we live. Religion that abides within the world inside.

This, then, the world inside ourselves, the exploration of this inner world, this is the great adventure of a lifetime, the pith and quick of everything. And the only way into this inner world is to go by means of dreams. Dreams are the way unto the light.

Dreams carry us into our own internal world where we find at last our own distinct existence, at its very best, at its most intense, full of passion, full of promise, full of noble purpose.

Dreams carry us beyond ourselves into the world of spirit and religion.

Then, because of dreams, we live a better life than we have lived before. A richer, finer, fuller life than we have known before. And our lives embody every day the spirit of religion.

So for those of you who hunger so and thirst for spirit, and have it not within your lives, turn then to your dreams.

If you would change your life, rearrange your life, look within your dreams.

If you would old life set aside, new life to liberate inside, work within your dreams.

If you would retrieve your life, achieve your life before you sell your bones, gather ye your dreams.

Yes, gather ye your dreams like diamonds,
which they truly are.

Diamonds of the Night.

And so fill up your life
with spirit and religion.

◊　　◊　　◊　　◊

The divine child fights the serpent

ABOUT THE PICTURES

THE PICTURES IN THIS BOOK are detail from photographs taken by the author of several paintings and two sculptures. The prints of the author's pictures were scanned into computer form and then cropped, sized, combined, enhanced, and otherwise manipulated by computer by the author for inclusion in the book. These pictures are presented here for educational and didactic purposes so as to demonstrate dramatically and graphically the psychological ideas that to the author were compelling in the various works of art.

COMMENTS OR DREAMS FROM READERS

THE AUTHOR WELCOMES comments or dreams from readers. Letters may be sent to the author in care of the publisher or by fax to 310-284-5761. The author's voice-mail is 415-322-8016 or 310-284-3401. Electronic mail may be directed to jameshagan@juno.com.

About the Book

The text of this book is set in twelve point type in the Garamond typeface with sixteen points of leading between the lines. Chapter titles are set in sixteen points, epigraphs in eleven. This book has been printed in both hard cover and paperback editions.

The typeface in the book was first cut by Claude Garamond in France in the sixteenth century. The Garamond family of type has long been noted for its beauty and elegance of style, and for its ease of reading. Over the years, this typeface has gone through many variations. More recently, Adobe Systems, Inc., the company that created Postscript™ computer fonts, converted the Garamond typeface into a printer font known as Adobe Garamond which was used to design and to print this book.

About the Publisher

PAGEMILL PRESS PUBLISHES BOOKS in the field of psychology and personal growth. Its authors explore the intellectual, psychological, and spiritual dimensions of our daily lives, such as the connection between mind and body, the power of myth and dreams in everyday circumstances, the role of the unconscious in human interactions, and the integration of a more complete experience of the body into life's activities.

PAGEMILL PRESS seeks to honor the writer's craft by nurturing the interior impulse to create, and by producing books that encourage a reader's intellectual and spiritual exploration. PAGEMILL PRESS regards highly the collaboration of publisher, editor, and author, and the creative expression that results for readers.

For a catalog of the publications of PAGEMILL PRESS, for editorial submissions, or for queries to the author, please direct correspondence to:

PAGEMILL PRESS   Telephone: (510) 848-3600
2716 Ninth Street   Facsimile: (510) 848-1326
Berkeley, CA 94710   E-mail: Circulus@aol.com
        Website: www.ReadersNdex.com/pagemill

About the Author

JAMES HAGAN IS A PSYCHOLOGIST in California. He was born in Kansas City, Missouri, in January, 1935, and grew up in Sherman, Texas, in the Red River Valley north of Dallas. Dr. Hagan received a Bachelor of Arts degree with honors from the University of Oklahoma in 1957. While at OU, Dr. Hagan was a member of its National Championship football team and was also elected to Phi Beta Kappa. After his graduation, Dr. Hagan served for five years in the United States Marine Corps as a jet fighter pilot of supersonic aircraft.

In 1962, Dr. Hagan left the Marine Corps for law school at Stanford University in Palo Alto, California. He received the degree of Juris Doctor in 1964. He has lived and worked in Palo Alto since that time. Dr. Hagan was married and is the father of three children.

In 1979, Dr. Hagan began the study of psychology at the Psychological Studies Institute in Palo Alto. He received his Ph.D. degree in 1985. After internship and examinations, in 1988 Dr. Hagan was licensed as a clinical psychologist in California. Dr. Hagan maintains a residence and office in both Palo Alto and Los Angeles. He is engaged in analytic work by means of dreams with clients throughout California.